The SCReeNWRiTiNG FORMuLa

The SCReeNWRiTiNG FORMULa

Why It Works and How to Use It

WRITER'S DIGEST BOOKS
www.writersdigest.com
Cincinnati, Ohio

RoB ToBiN

Visit our Web sites at www.writersdigest.com and www.wdeditors.com for information on more resources for writers.

To receive a free weekly e-mail newsletter delivering tips and updates about writing and about Writer's Digest products, register directly at our Web site at http://newsletters.fwpublications.com.

11   10   09   08   07   5 4 3 2 1

Distributed in Canada by Fraser Direct, 100 Armstrong Avenue, Georgetown, ON, Canada L7G 5S4, Tel: (905) 877-4411; Distributed in the U.K. and Europe by David & Charles, Brunel House, Newton Abbot, Devon, TQ12 4PU, England, Tel: (+44) 1626 323200, Fax: (+44) 1626 323319, E-mail: postmaster@davidandcharles.co.uk; Distributed in Australia by Capricorn Link, P.O. Box 704, Windsor, NSW 2756 Australia, Tel: (02) 4577-3555

Library of Congress Cataloging-in-Publication Data

Tobin, Rob, 1957-
  The Screenwriting Formula: why it works and how to use it / Rob Tobin.
-- 1st ed.
    p. cm.
  ISBN 978-1-58297-462-0 (pbk. : alk. paper)
  1. Motion picture authorship. I. Title.
  PN1996.T59 2007
  808.2'3--dc22

                                    2006035173

Edited by Amy Schell
Designed by Claudean Wheeler
Production coordinated by Mark Griffin

TO MY FAMILY:

Leslie, George, Marie, John,
Brian, and Josiah

They inspired more than my writing;
they inspired my life.

ABOUT THE AUTHOR

Rob Tobin's latest script, *Camel Wars*, was written using the techniques and principles in this book. *Creative Screenwriting* magazine recently produced two of Rob's instructional DVDs. He has read more than 5,000 screenplays as a reader and development exec, and his books and DVDs are based in large part on what he saw in those scripts—the good, the bad, and the ugly. Rob's philosophy is summed up in a single sentence: "Writing well isn't just a goal, it's a responsibility."

CoNTeNTS

1: THE SEVEN ELEMENTS

2: THE STRUCTURE

3: THE BIG PICTURE

> *"If brevity be the soul of wit, then tonight*
> *we shall be very witty."*
> —BILLY CRYSTAL, MC-ING THE ACADEMY AWARDS

> *"Show it, don't say it."*
> —TENET OF GOOD SCREENWRITING

The title of this book says it all: There is a formula for writing screenplays, a formula used to write nearly every successful movie in Hollywood history. This book will teach you what the formula is and how to use it to write structurally perfect scripts with believable dialogue, credible and interesting characters, a strong but unobtrusive theme, and the kind of story that sticks in the minds of readers and viewers.

You'll note that this is a relatively short book, because the point is to get you writing as quickly as possible. In fact,

---

I invite you to skip the introduction and go right to Chapter 1, so that you can start learning and applying the tools of your trade immediately.

In the meantime, in the spirit of Billy Crystal, let's get witty, and let's get down to business.

A few more things before we really begin (sorry, Billy): Making a feature film is one of mankind's most amazing accomplishments. It takes hundreds and sometimes thousands of skilled professionals, using creative brilliance, technological genius, mind-boggling computer power, and millions, tens of millions or sometimes even *hundreds* of millions of dollars, and the kind of time and resources to rival the greatest projects in human history.

Watch The Lord of the Rings trilogy and try to imagine what it took to put it on screen, *one shot at a time*. Or consider *Godzilla*, the 1998 American version starring Matthew Broderick. It wasn't much of a movie in terms of quality, and it has already been bashed enough by critics. But watch it yourself and try to imagine what it took to put even *that* clunker on screen. It's astonishing.

In this book, when I pan a movie, I am panning it for being badly written. I'm panning the producers for choosing a bad script; the writers for writing a bad script; the script doctors for rewriting a bad script and still managing to keep it bad; and even the director for being too ignorant about a story to choose a better script to direct.

But in the end, the making of a film is like the building of a skyscraper. The skyscraper might turn out to be another arid, ugly, high-rise monstrosity, but it still takes an enormous amount of skill and collaborative effort to build that ugly seventy-story building.

So too with feature films: Even badly written ones take an enormous—nearly *miraculous*—amount of work, skill, ambition, experience, time, attention to detail, blood, sweat, tears, frustration, and heartbreak to bring to the big screen.

I tip my hat and bow deeply to the people with the courage to even try making a film. And...I suggest they read this book before making their *next* movies. Because as Oliver Stone said: "You can make a bad movie from a good script, but you can't make a good movie from a bad script."

Enjoy the read, use the tools and techniques herein, and Good Writing to you all!

ROB TOBIN
HUNTINGTON BEACH, CALIFORNIA
JUNE, 2007

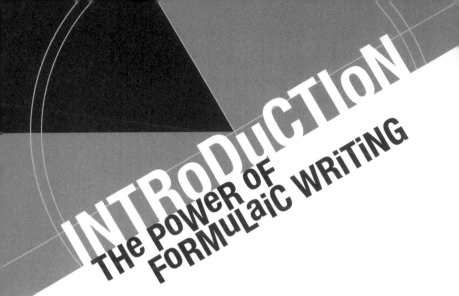

INTRODUCTION
THE POWER OF FORMULAIC WRITING

"His writing was formulaic."

"Television has become so formulaic that there's nothing worth watching anymore."

"That movie was so formulaic."

The next time someone calls your work formulaic, say thank you, and tell them to buy this book.

"Formulaic" has become a pejorative term when applied to the arts and especially to the art of writing. But let me ask you: If someone gave you the formula for turning lead into gold, would you take it? Or would you self-righteously proclaim that gold created through the use of a formula is not worth having?

For those of you who would refuse the gold, I suggest you race back to your bookstore and get a refund on this book.

This book is specifically about learning and using a formula to create all kinds of gold—both figurative and literal.

There is a screenwriting formula. Most commercially and critically successful screenplays use some variation of this formula. If you want screenwriting success, artistic and/or commercial, the first step is for you to become aware of this formula. Learn it backward and forward, and then apply it with your own unique voice, style, personality, goals, and philosophies.

The formula consists of knowing what the elements of a screenplay are and how to use them. A screenplay consists of seven basic story elements. These seven elements are:

- The Hero
- The Hero's Character Flaw
- Enabling Circumstances
- The Opponent
- The Hero's Ally
- The Life-Changing Event
- Jeopardy

These seven elements, combined with specific structural elements, constitute the screenwriting formula. We'll talk more about what these elements are and how to use them as we go on.

CHANGING THE FORMULA

Can you change the formula, or fiddle with it, or disregard it altogether? Yes, yes, and yes, although the results will vary, depending on your level of writing skill.

Masters of any art can flagrantly disregard the rules or create new ones based on their talents: Picasso, Stravinsky,

Hemingway, Samuel Beckett, and Charlie Kaufman are examples that come to mind. But for the rest of us, formulaic writing enhanced by our individual voices and personalities can be the key to success.

This book will give you everything you need to know about the elements that go into a well-written, structurally sound screenplay.

BADLY WRITTEN FILMS CAN MAKE MONEY

As already mentioned, there are a lot of lousy scripts that get made into movies. Some of these lousy movies do very well, sometimes even extraordinarily well, at the box office. The screenplay for the 1997 film *Titanic* is so weak that it was not even nominated for an Oscar, even though the film itself made more than $2 *billion* worldwide and won eleven Oscars!

However, unless you have a $250 million dollar budget, James Cameron as director, and Leonardo DiCaprio under contract to star, the best way to get someone to read and produce your writing is to make sure it's the best writing it can be.

BAD FILMS AREN'T FORMULAIC— AND THAT'S THE PROBLEM!

Most of the films and television shows that people call "formulaic" actually *fail* to follow the formula outlined in this book. In fact, they tend not to follow any formula whatsoever.

Such infamously deficient screenplays as *Titanic*, *Hudson Hawk*, and *Ishtar* were tremendously weak in terms of the hero, opponent, hero's ally, character flaw, life-changing event, subjective storyline, and final battle scene—all elements described in this book.

So when someone calls a work "formulaic," you can respond: "No, it's not. Because if it had followed a formula, it would have been a better movie."

Maybe the problem is that people, including filmmakers, think of screenwriting as an art, like sculpture or painting. The truth, however, is that screenwriting is more like architecture than like painting. Architecture combines science and art. It deals with rigid structures and flowing lines, beauty and serviceability, style and structure. This is exactly what a well-written screenplay does—it combines the rigid with the flowing, style with structure, beauty and serviceability. If it *doesn't* combine these aspects, it is likely a FAILED screenplay.

Look at it this way—a screenplay is a like a cup. It is also what goes *into* the cup, whether it is the finest wine or the cheapest red eye. What you *drink* is the wine, but the way in which the wine is *delivered* to you is the cup. Without the cup, the wine spills onto the floor, unavailable to you. The cup is structure. The wine is creativity — *your* creativity.

Drinking glasses and cups come in an infinite variety of shapes, sizes, and colors. However, there are certain minimum requirements in order for a cup to be functional. For instance, a cup with sides sloping downward probably won't hold your wine very well. A cup with holes in the sides and bottom is not great for holding anything. So too with story structure—you have a lot of room to "play" with it and be creative, but there are certain minimum requirements.

A well-structured "cup" (screenplay) delivers the writer's "wine" (creativity, message, point of view, etc.) to his or her audience. It's up to the writer to create a palatable wine.

However, it doesn't matter how wonderful the wine tastes unless there's some type of vessel to contain the wine and let us drink it.

The most beautiful, creative, unconventional, free-spirited building in the world is held up by a scientifically designed structure. Similarly, even the wildest movie is held up by a very carefully designed structure.

Story structure *is* formulaic! It had better be, if it's to successfully hold your story. Even the quirkiest Frank Lloyd Wright home is held together by mundane framing, two-by-fours, and wooden beams in a specific (formulaic) pattern, with studs so many inches apart, and with so many nails, joints, and joists. Even the wildest Charlie Kaufman story (*Eternal Sunshine of the Spotless Mind* or *Adaptation*) is held together by traditional story components and relationships such as the ones discussed in this book.

I recently engaged in a debate with a movie critic who loved M. Knight Shyamalan's *The Village*. It was fine with me that he liked it on an emotional level. However, when this critic admitted that he liked the movie based *solely* on his emotional reaction to it, he unwittingly admitted to doing a huge disservice to his readers. This critic went so far as to say that he was a critic not because he knew anything *about* films, but because he *liked* films. Don't be that guy or girl! Know story structure and how stories are put together, even if you decide to put your story together in a completely unconventional way.

NOTE: If you play with convention, you're creative. If you don't know what the conventions are, you're too lazy to have learned your craft.

Pablo Picasso began as a traditional painter with all of the traditional skills, including the ability to create and use perspective, lighting, shadow, heaviness of stroke, and color. When he put thirteen breasts on one side of a one-dimensional woman's face (okay, a slight exaggeration), he didn't do so because he'd never seen a naked woman. It wasn't that Picasso didn't know how to create the impression of depth, or didn't know basic biology and anatomy. He knew what the "rules" were and he decided to break them in order to achieve a very specific effect. In fact, before becoming an abstract artist, Picasso was a *very accomplished* traditional painter. His father, an art teacher, taught little Pablo traditional painting skills.

It's interesting to note that Picasso's *Self-Portrait With Uncombed Hair* from 1896 shows the brilliant painter as an unruly looking young man, but in a completely traditional portrait style. His *Self-Portrait* from 1972 shows what looks like a space alien after having been exposed to high-level nuclear radiation, as seen through a camera lens that had been warped by being left out in the sun too long. The second portrait would not have been possible for Picasso had he not learned how to paint the first conventional portrait. One of my editors remarked that Picasso had done the second painting in *crayon*. Now *that* is liberation; the ability to throw all the rules away, based on an absolute knowledge of those rules and of the consequences of throwing those rules away or altering them.

If for no other reason than to know the rules you're breaking, *learn* what the rules are and what traditional structure is. It will prevent that fancy parquet floor of yours from collapsing and taking the rest of the house with it, simply because you didn't know the formula for creating stress-bearing framing or a stress-bearing storyline.

As I asked earlier, if someone offered you the formula for turning lead into gold, would you take it? Or would you pooh-pooh it as "formulaic" and thus beneath you? Check out the kind of gold that traditional story structure has created, before you throw that structure out.

REMEMBER: Every element of storytelling emerges from the structure of the story, in the same way that every element of a house (even the most artistic) emerges from the structure of the house.

Remember those story elements I mentioned a few pages ago? In the following chapters, we will describe each of these elements and give examples from classic and recent films. Then we'll build our own little story from *scratch*, based on these elements and other structural elements. This book will show you that it *can* be done, *how* it can be done, and the *ease* with which it can be done, simply by using the techniques and information contained in this book.

THe SeVeN STORY ELEMENTS

1

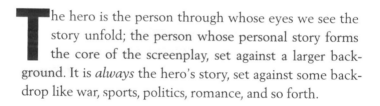

1. THe HeRO

The hero is the person through whose eyes we see the story unfold; the person whose personal story forms the core of the screenplay, set against a larger background. It is *always* the hero's story, set against some backdrop like war, sports, politics, romance, and so forth.

FULLY DRAWN CHARACTERS

The traditional hero of old was the white-hatted (and white-skinned) guy with blindingly white teeth who was always nice to old ladies and polite to young ladies. He was protective of the town's citizens and had no apparent flaw in his character.

This old-time hero was fearless even in the face of an army of bad guys. He was never tempted by the big-breasted, long-legged saloon girl and never at a loss for words, and he never, ever went to the bathroom.

Good writers do not make their heroes like these old-time "white hats" anymore, unless they're doing a farce like *Blazing Saddles*. Writers know they need a flawed hero, because the story will be about a hero struggling to overcome a flaw in order to achieve a worthwhile goal against significant opposition.

This may sound simplistic, even trite, but it forms the basis for just about every well-written film ever made.

Tobin's Dinner Test

We need a hero who is either sympathetic or interesting enough for us to pay ten dollars at the movie theater to hear his story.

I call this my "dinner test" because if I don't want to have dinner with the hero of a movie, then why would I want to spend ten bucks (not counting popcorn, licorice, and soda) to sit for two hours to watch him in a darkened movie theater?

Of course, we can have an evil hero such as Tim Robbins' character in *The Player*, because although Robbins' character isn't likable, he is *interesting*. Remember that even the word "hero" is a bit misleading since the main character of a movie is not always likable, strong, or heroic. *Midnight Cowboy*, *The Player*, *The Verdict*, and *Crash* are all classic examples of films in which the main characters are clearly anti-heroic.

In order for us to want to follow the hero through a two-hour movie, he may not have to be likable, but he'd damned well better be *interesting*. Interesting enough for us to want to have a two-hour dinner with him in order to hear his story.

EXAMPLES FROM FAMOUS FILMS

Watching a hero struggle with his flaw makes for an interesting film. For example, Frankie is the hero of *Million Dollar Baby*. It is through his eyes that we see the story unfold. It is his personal story of overcoming the fear and guilt that losing his daughter has created in him.

John is the hero of *Wedding Crashers*. We follow him through the story. We cheer for him, and he is the one who makes the decision in the end that saves him or damns him.

Ennis is the hero of *Brokeback Mountain*. This film is a tragedy because the hero does not overcome his primary flaw. Like many classic tragedies, however, it is by failing to change his flaw that Ennis recognizes opportunities he would have missed otherwise, which allows the film to end on a hopeful note.

Rocky Balboa is the hero of *Rocky*. It is his personal story of overcoming his self-identification as a "loser"; it takes place against the background of the world of boxing.

In the brilliant *Secrets & Lies*, the mother, Cynthia (played magnificently by Brenda Blethyn), is the hero. Her story is set against the backdrop of a disintegrating lower-class British family. Though the film is filled with strong, interesting characters, this is Cynthia's personal story and it is through her eyes that we see the story unfold.

Schindler's List was Schindler's story, played out against the backdrop of the Holocaust. It was the hero's story that made *Schindler's List* different from *Sophie's Choice*, which was itself different from other Holocaust movies. It is the uniqueness of the hero's story that makes one film different from another film in the same genre.

It's important to remember that it's the *hero's story* you are telling, because you might be tempted to write a "tornado story." In that case, you are writing about the backdrop, not the hero. A story, to most of us humans, is a story of a human (or an anthropomorphized creature that functions as a human), and the struggle that that human has to go through in order to become a better person in the face of great jeopardy—emotional and/or physical. Storms may move (a lot!) but emotionally and spiritually they are inanimate objects, not human beings or anything resembling human beings. Storms don't struggle, they just *are*. They have no flaws to overcome, and no way to overcome them.

Certainly you can write about a storm, or about football, or about the ocean or outer space, it'll just be very difficult to make an interesting story of it. However, put a human being in front of the backdrop and the story pops out at you. *Titanic* isn't about the Titanic; *Twister* isn't about a tornado. Both films are about the people, whether these people are standing against the backdrop of a sinking ship or of an approaching tornado. People make the story.

Another problem is that if you're writing about a tornado, there is nothing to distinguish your story from other "bad weather" stories. *Rocky, Million Dollar Baby, Requiem for*

"*All right, Mr. DeMille, I'm ready for my close-up.*"
—SUNSET BLVD.

"*May the Force be with you.*"
—STAR WARS

"*I love the smell of napalm in the morning.*"
—APOCALYPSE NOW

"*E.T. phone home.*"
—E.T. THE EXTRA-TERRESTRIAL

a Heavyweight, and *The Champ* are all boxing stories. If the stories were *about* boxing, they'd all be pretty much the same. After all, how many ways can you describe a left hook or an uppercut? The stories of the *heroes* are what distinguish these films from each other.

There are some good examples of stories that are not necessarily hero-based. One *backdrop* story is the Oscar-winning *Crash*. Written by Canadian Paul Haggis (*Million Dollar Baby*), *Crash* is about racism rather than the story of a hero set against a *backdrop* of racism. One major critic called *Crash* one of the worst films ever to win an Oscar; that is precisely because Haggis wrote about the backdrop instead of the hero.

If you're going to write a "tornado story," make it, instead, the story of a fascinating character overcoming a compelling character flaw, set against the *backdrop* of a tornado.

This is a crucial point. Developing your hero is the most important part of writing an interesting, compelling, commercially and critically viable screenplay. When most people think of a film they like, they think of the hero: Rick Blaine in *Casablanca*, Josh in *Big*, Forrest Gump in *Forrest Gump*, the robot in *Terminator 2*, M'Lynn Eatonton in *Steel Magnolias*, Suzanne Vale in *Postcards from the Edge*, Sophie Zawistowski in *Sophie's Choice*, or Frank Horrigan in *In the Line of Fire*.

If you can't remember who the hero was in a particular movie, I'll bet you didn't like the movie much—the hero's story IS the movie!

LET'S BUILD A STORY FROM SCRATCH ...

In the film industry, screenplays usually have three acts: Act One is approximately thirty pages, Act Two is sixty pages, and Act Three is thirty pages. This is because the first filmmakers at the beginning of the twentieth century took their cue from "legitimate theater." If stageplays had three acts, then filmmakers supposed that screenplays should, too.

When dealing with anyone from the entertainment industry, you should still refer to the three-act structure. This is because the other person will become confused or irritated by your use of four acts. I use four segments here as a modification of the three-act structure, and for instructional purposes only. The middle act is divided into the first part of the second act and the second part of the second act.) As I mentioned before, each segment is usually about thirty pages long, but this can vary greatly for various reasons.

We'll call the hero Ross Parkes. We don't know much about Ross because we haven't yet decided on the other six elements, but let's give him a bit of an identity. Ross is obviously male, and let's go with American, late thirties to early forties; his race isn't relevant. If nothing else, he should be easy to cast!

CHALLENGING ROLES ATTRACT GOOD ACTORS

Creating strong roles in your screenplay doesn't mean that you should make any of your characters impossible to portray. However, do give each major character the kind of scenes that, if acted well, will bring acclaim for managing such a challenging role. Actors often tell their agents to look for "Oscar roles" for them. They mean roles that will stretch them enough so that critics will be impressed. Think of *Forrest Gump*, *Silence of the Lambs*, *Gandhi*, and *Charlie*—all difficult roles that earned the actors Oscars.

Leading roles aren't, of course, the only roles that should be challenging. The choice of the hero's ally is important in the process of casting and "packaging" a movie. Packaging means attaching big name stars and/or a director to a script before going in to pitch the script to producers or executives.

If you create both an interesting hero *and* hero's ally, you'll have a better chance of attracting actors who can help you sell the movie.

Million Dollar Baby is a perfect example. The ally, Scrap, played by Morgan Freeman, is a great role—so great, in fact, that the truly venerable actor Mr. Freeman won an Oscar for it.

Many other notable actors won their Oscars for supporting rather than leading roles. Whoopi Goldberg should have won for her leading role in *The Color Purple*, but instead won for playing the ally in *Ghost*.

Denzel Washington won his first Oscar for a supporting role in *Glory*.

Making the ally's role as strong as you can helps not only in writing the script, but also in marketing it afterwards.

2. THE FLAW

The hero usually has a flaw at the beginning of the story. This flaw hinders him (or her) in some way, even if the hero doesn't realize what the flaw is—or that it is hindering him.

The hero most often views his flaw as a defense mechanism he needs for his survival. The hero does not view his flaw as a flaw, but as a way of coping with life, as a behavior that protects his life metaphorically or perhaps even literally. That is why the hero has not already let go of his flaw—he actually does believe that he needs it.

This is an important component of your story; it creates intrinsic conflict and tension. Why? Because all stories are essentially about a hero who has to overcome his flaw in order to accomplish some worthwhile goal. Thus the hero—and the audience—feels an innate conflict in having to choose between the flaw that he feels is necessary for his survival, and the worthwhile goal.

EXAMPLES FROM FAMOUS FILMS

In the Oscar-winning *Million Dollar Baby*, Clint Eastwood's Frankie is the hero. It's through his eyes that we see the story unfold. His flaw is that he refuses to become involved with people, to commit personally to any relationship. This flaw arises from an unexplained rift with his daughter and also, perhaps, from guilt over a fight in which Eddie "Scrap-Iron" Dupris (played by Morgan Freeman) lost more than the round. Frankie feels responsible because he failed to stop the fight in time to save Scrap's eye. This flaw, a fear of intimacy, robs Frankie of the chance for intimacy, but also protects him from getting hurt again, as he did in the fallout with his daughter.

Frankie will never be able to train Maggie well enough for her to challenge for the women's world boxing championship until he is able to overcome his own fear of intimacy. For Frankie to successfully train Maggie, he has to get close to her, and that is exactly what he has spent so many years avoiding: getting close to anyone. To be successful with Maggie on the level of boxing, he has to give her everything he has, not only as a manager but as a father figure.

We see Frankie's doubts and fears expressed when he refuses to let Big Willie fight for the championship for fear of hurting the young boxer. As a result, he loses Big Willie to another promoter who does get Big Willie a title shot, which he wins, becoming a world champion.

Scrap, Morgan Freeman's character, tells Frankie exactly what his problem is in two bits of dialogue. "Ain't about connections. 'Bout you not believing in him." Then, a few seconds later as Frankie argues with him, Scrap says, "You just protected yourself right out of a championship fight."

This is exactly what a flaw does for and to a hero: It protects him, but prevents him from gaining something valuable.

In *Batman Begins*, Bruce Wayne cannot become a superhero and save Gotham until he overcomes his guilt over his parents' death and steps up with the confidence he'll need to battle his former ally and teacher, Henri Ducard.

In *Brokeback Mountain*, the hero Ennis is paralyzed by fear. As a child he was led by his father to a drainage ditch to see the brutally beaten corpse of a gay man, and his father told Ennis that this is what happens to "faggots." Ennis quite rightly fears being killed for being gay himself, and it is a fear that protects him from risking his life by "outing" himself. Unfortunately, it also keeps him from having the kind of relationship that his gay lover Jack offers him, and he ends up living alone because of that flaw.

In *Rocky*, another Oscar-winning boxing film, Rocky Balboa defines himself as a loser because his father told him that he was stupid. This flaw keeps Rocky on the streets of Philadelphia, working for mobsters, hanging

"They call me Mister Tibbs!"

—IN THE HEAT OF THE NIGHT

"I'm as mad as hell, and I'm not going to take this anymore!"

—NETWORK

"Well, there are certain sections of New York, Major, that I wouldn't advise you try to invade."

—CASABLANCA

"I am big! It's the pictures that got small."

—SUNSET BLVD.

around other losers, without a romantic relationship, without a future, and without even trying to take advantage of his boxing potential.

Rocky's flaw is his lack of self-esteem. However, from Rocky's point of view, it's the best way to cope with life. His lack of self-esteem keeps him from getting into situations he can't handle. That's why he doesn't train harder. If he started to succeed a little, it would put him in front of more people, raise expectations, and of course, the inevitable would happen—he'd lose and prove his father right. Staying at the level of club fights, competing only against other losers, Rocky has his best chance of not being found out. Thus in his mind, his flaw protects him from even greater hurt than he has already experienced.

In *Hook*, the adult Peter Pan has suppressed his inner child because he believes this is what allows him to hold on to the "adult" world in which he and his family live. He believes that being Peter Pan would cause him to lose this "human" and "adult" world. This fear causes him to forget who he really is and keeps him tied to the material world of overwork and neglect of his family. He has to choose between his flaw, which is a type of self-induced amnesia, and the opportunity to rescue his family from Captain Hook.

OUR STORY

Okay, so what is our hero Ross's flaw? Let's go with the same flaw that drives so many heroes: fear. Just as Frankie in *Million Dollar Baby* is afraid of intimacy and Ennis in *Brokeback Mountain* is afraid of being "found out," Ross is afraid of the world finding out who he really is. And who is he? Well, why don't we go with the obvious —Ross is a coward, and he is afraid of people finding *out* that he's a coward.

Now the next question is: Why would Ross consider cowardice a good thing, a defense mechanism that protects him in some very important way? Well…fear keeps Ross from doing dangerous things, right? If he doesn't do dangerous things, he won't screw up.

So maybe Ross is like Rocky: He's afraid of being put into a situation he can't handle. Maybe in the past he failed to handle some kind of situation well. Let's say he performed an act of cowardice—let's say he was in the military and froze in the middle of combat. His *continuing* fear keeps him from the kind of situations where he might once again expose his cowardice.

Similarly, in *Million Dollar Baby*, Frankie's fear of intimacy has its roots in his failure to have an intimate relationship with his daughter. In both cases, the heroes use their flaws to avoid repeating previous mistakes.

But we want our hero Ross to be more than just a coward. We don't want it to be laughable if and when he "snaps out of it" and tries to do something heroic. In other words, a cowardly little dentist, accountant, or gardener who has no experience whatsoever with violence or action, would not make a believable action hero even if he found a way to overcome his cowardice.

So here's what we do: We show that our hero is more than just frightened little Ross. How do we show this? Well, maybe the boss asks Ross to make the daily cash deposit, something usually done by another employee.

We see Ross carrying a large sum of money to a bank, with darkness falling. We see his fear. Our frightened Ross, holding the moneybag as darkness falls, glances this way and that. He perspires and breathes heavily.

Sure enough, he's jumped by a group of men who have been tailing him. But instead of folding, Ross beats the hell out of the thugs! How could he do this? Because he's a former Green Beret! Yes, he's a coward, but he's also Rambo, and, when attacked, he acts on instinct.

Ross takes out the thugs. Maybe he gets slightly wounded, which doesn't stop him or even slow him down. But, at the end of the fight, Ross stands triumphant, but also scared out of his wits, gasping, sweating, glancing around, paranoid. He rushes to the night deposit box, shoves the day's deposits in, and races back to his car. He locks the car doors and roars away in a panic.

Ross is physically capable, but something else is happening inside that makes him unreasonably afraid.

This is an intriguing way to introduce Ross and his flaw, and it pulls viewers in. They'll want to stick around at least long enough to find out why this Rambo character is scared of his shadow.

3. ENaBLiNG CiRCUMSTaNCeS

E nabling circumstances are the circumstances that the hero creates or finds for himself; they are the circumstances that surround the hero at the beginning of the story and that *allow him to maintain his flaw*. Remember, the hero views his flaw as a defense mechanism, something necessary for his survival. Thus it's natural for the hero to seek out or create a set of *circumstances* (a job, a neighborhood, a set of friends, et al.) that *enables* him to maintain that critically important flaw.

EXAMPLES FROM FAMOUS FILMS

In *Hook*, the grown-up Peter Pan, having foresworn Neverland and his own inner child, surrounds himself with everything that is anti-Neverland: the world of the corporate raider, surrounded by other A-type, ultra-serious businessmen.

Think of *Wedding Crashers*. John and Jeremy are petrified of marriage or any other romantic commitment. So where

"A census taker once tried to test me. I ate his liver with some fava beans and a nice Chianti."

—THE SILENCE OF THE LAMBS

"Where'd they teach you to talk like this—some Panama City 'Sailor want to hump-hump bar?' Or was today getaway day and your last shot at his whiskey? Sell crazy someplace else—we're all stocked up here."

—AS GOOD AS IT GETS.

"Louis, I think this is the beginning of a beautiful friendship."

—CASABLANCA

do they work? In a law firm that specializes in divorce! And what do they do for recreation? They crash weddings for one-night stands with girls, lying about who they are—in other words, their entire world is set up to avoid intimacy and to deep-six any intimacy that might sneak through their defenses. It's the perfect set of circumstances to enable them to maintain their flaw, which is their belief that marriage is "our punishment for original sin" (Jeremy's line from one of the earlier drafts of *Wedding Crashers*).

Another powerful example is Rocky Balboa, living on the streets of Philadelphia, training in the worst boxing gyms, working for two-bit mobsters, fighting two-bit opponents, and refusing help from coaches like Burgess Meredith's character, Mickey. In this environment, Rocky can continue as a loser, and he can avoid situations in which he might embarrass himself. It protects him from having unrealistic expectations or opportunities. It keeps him from doing things that a "loser" shouldn't even *try* to do.

Enabling circumstances also help the audience accept the hero's flaw and thus the hero's credibility.

Imagine Frankie from *Million Dollar Baby* as a social worker or psychologist. A profession like that demands deep involvement with the lives of other people and carries the risk of making mistakes that could ruin those lives in the way Frankie ruined his relationship with his own daughter. Frankie's flaw is that he doesn't *want* to get involved, doesn't want to risk the intimacy he had with his daughter, an intimacy that nearly destroyed him when it went wrong.

Imagine Peter living in Neverland. Try as he might to be grown up and to suppress his inner child, it wouldn't work, not when he was surrounded by the childlike magic of Neverland, with the Lost Boys and Captain Hook and all those adventures awaiting him.

Imagine John or Jeremy from *Wedding Crashers* running a dating service. Or a wedding chapel.

Imagine Rocky growing up in Bel-Air, Malibu, or Beverly Hills as a wealthy man driving a $150,000 car and heir to a huge fortune. Those circumstances wouldn't allow the hero to identify himself as a loser. More importantly, the audience wouldn't *believe* that the hero could maintain that kind of flaw in those circumstances. You would lose your audience from the outset. The enabling circumstances allow the hero to maintain his flaw and allow the audience to maintain its belief in the hero and his flaw.

OUR STORY

Ross, the self-proclaimed coward, needs a situation and a job that will not demand any courage from him and where he will not stand out.

Whether it's fair or not, accountants do not have a reputation for being adrenalin junkies. So our hero will be an innocuous accountant, with nothing expected of him in terms of courage or daring.

Think about it: Our hero, the former Green Beret, once made a decision that got a lot of people killed. Why? Because that is the nature of war—mistakes can be fatal.

If I had made a mistake that led to someone's death, I might have decided to go to work in the least threatening, least dangerous, least physically demanding environment I could find. As an accountant, I can make a mistake with figures but it won't kill anyone, and it can be corrected. It's as safe as you can get—not just for me, but for the people I work with.

You see, after making a mistake that killed someone, I would want to stop making mistakes. That's not possible for a human being—to stop making mistakes. The next best thing is to find a place where mistakes don't hurt anyone.

I suppose Ross could have taken up working on an assembly line or digging ditches … anything that allows him the smallest possible chance of hurting someone with his mistakes—again.

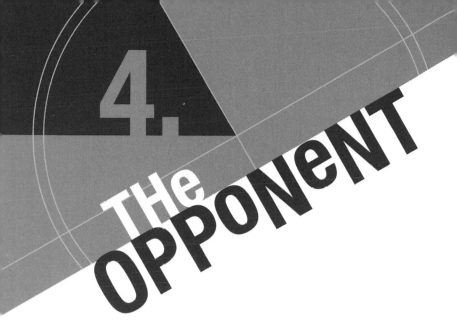

4. The OPPONENT

In simplest terms, the opponent is someone who opposes the hero getting or doing or being what he wants. The opponent is the one who believably and effectively opposes the hero in achieving his main goal. The opponent is not necessarily or even ideally a "bad guy," but rather someone standing between the hero and some important goal. The opponent is sometimes even a "good guy." An example is *The Fugitive* in which Tommy Lee Jones plays the opponent. He's a good cop just doing his job. It is also important to note, however, that the opponent can be the same as an *ally*; sometimes, preventing the hero from getting what he wants is what forces him to let go of his flaw.

In fact, the opponent can be someone who has the hero's best interest at heart—someone who is, in fact, also the hero's ally. The combined opponent/ally character is most common in love stories and in romantic comedies.

"I'm going to make him an offer he can't refuse."

—THE GODFATHER

"You don't understand! I coulda' had class. I coulda' been a contender. I could've been somebody, instead of a bum, which is what I am."

—ON THE WATERFRONT

"Here's looking at you, kid."

—CASABLANCA

An example is *When Harry Met Sally*. Sally, played by Meg Ryan, is the opponent because she opposes Harry, played by Billy Crystal. He desires to keep friendship and love separate; she wants to combine them. When Harry realizes Sally is right, he is able to attain a much more worthwhile goal: being in love with her.

This is an important point. What the hero wants at the beginning of the movie is not always in his own best interest, and the person who opposes the hero in getting what he wants sometimes acts in the hero's best interest. These kinds of opponents are often much more interesting than the trite "black-hatted and black-hearted" villains of those corny old westerns and war movies.

Another extremely important point: The opponent is the person who instigates the life-changing event, the event that occurs at the end of the first act (more on that in Chapter 6).

DIFFERENT KINDS OF OPPONENTS

In *Forrest Gump*, the opponent was Jenny, played by Robin Wright. Not only is Jenny not a "bad guy," she is a wonderful, caring person who Forrest dearly loves. She is fully drawn, a young woman trying to escape a horrific past of physical abuse by her father. How can this sweet young woman be the opponent? Because Forrest Gump's main desire, perhaps even his *only* desire, is to be with Jenny.

Jenny opposes Forrest's attempt to be with her by continually running away from her own past. In doing so, she runs from Forrest. Forrest ends up winning in the end by loving her so strongly and purely that she is forced to re alize that he is the right man for her. The tragedy is that, unfortunately, by then it's too late for them.

The Difference Between Opponents and Villains

It is important to note that there is a difference between the terms "opponent" and "villain."

Opponents are powerfully drawn, believable, intriguing, highly functional characters with their own believable motivations, flaws, and points of view.

Villains, on the other hand, are one-dimensional "bad guys" who most often exist in animated or live-action "cartoon" films such as *Superman*, *101 Dalmatians*, and *Ace Ventura: Pet Detective*, all of which were extremely successful and entertaining films, by the way, but none of which had depth or drama to them.

You can choose to have a villain in your story instead of a fully drawn opponent, especially if you're going to do a "cartoon" screenplay such as a broad farce or superhero action adventure. However, your chances of success will increase commensurate with the complexity and power of *all* your characters, especially the hero, hero's ally, and opponent. Even *Superman* would have been a more interesting movie with the use of an opponent rather than just a cardboard-cutout "nasty" villain.

A perfect example is the most recent Batman movie, *Batman Begins*, which was widely hailed as being the best of the franchise. This *Batman* movie created a strong opponent for Batman, an opponent who was much more strongly drawn than the Penguin or Joker of other *Batman* films. Instead of being just a "villain," Ducard is a unique, strongly drawn individual with a viable point of view.

EXAMPLES FROM FAMOUS FILMS

In *Wedding Crashers*, the opponent is Claire, the first woman John can't just "get rid of" or treat as a one-night stand: She is the woman who opposes him and his flaw.

In *Rocky*, the heavyweight champ Apollo Creed is the opponent, because he opposes Rocky in getting what he wants—to go the distance in the ring. He also opposes Rocky's desire to remain anonymous for fear of failing in public. How good is Apollo as an opponent? He forces Rocky into possibly failing in front of the entire television-viewing world! Now THAT is an opponent!

In *Million Dollar Baby*, Maggie is the opponent, because she's the one who insists that Frankie open up to her and risk caring about her. In short, Maggie is a female boxer with a lot of heart and no training or technique. It is that combination—her need for someone like Frankie and her huge heart—that end up being irresistible to Frankie. All of this is initiated by Maggie, the opponent, simply by her showing up in the gym and showing her courage, refusing to let Frankie reject or ignore her.

In most of our examples, we see that the opponent intentionally or inadvertently makes it difficult for the hero to maintain his flaw. In *Million Dollar Baby*, Maggie's goal is simply to get Frankie to train her. The result, however, is to force him to open up and risk an intimate (fatherly) relationship. Why is she successful? Because she is the perfect opponent for Frankie. She is female, roughly the same age as his daughter, and she enters into his world so willingly and completely that she negates the power of his enabling circumstances, circumstances that would normally keep women at bay.

Prior to Maggie showing up, the only people in Frankie's enabling circumstances were brutal men who made demands of him that he could easily meet without risking intimacy. It was a perfect set of enabling circumstances, but Frankie didn't expect Maggie to appear and tear those circumstances apart.

OUR STORY

So, who is *our* hero's opponent? Ross's opponent is someone who comes into his world and presents a threat so dangerous or an offer so tempting that it forces Ross to make a choice between his flaw and the threat or offer.

Let's say that the opponent is someone who is the opposite of Ross, someone fearless, macho—even belligerent. Someone strong enough to threaten the hero and perhaps to threaten other people, as well. This forces Ross to choose between remaining a coward and stepping forward to accept the opponent's challenge.

But remember, Ross is an accountant. What kind of seriously threatening opponent is going to enter Ross's placid world of numbers and tax deductions? Well, let's say that Ross works for a medium-sized or even smaller business. The opponent—let's call him Matt—is a mid-level management type. Matt's an ambitious, aggressive, business type, maybe unethical, as well. He starts making demands of his employees, including Ross. This gives us a skeleton on which to base Ross's opponent; it is easy to see how these two types of people would clash.

5. The Hero's ALLY

The hero's ally is the person who helps the hero overcome his flaw. This is the person the hero relies on, reluctantly or not, for help. It is also usually the person who spends the most on-screen time with the hero.

It's important to note that seldom does the *opponent* spend a significant amount of time with the hero, especially in the second act, unless the ally and the opponent are the same character, which, as noted earlier, is also a common plot device. Rather, it's the hero's ally who usually has the most on-screen time with the hero in the second act.

THE ALLY'S JOB

The ally's job is to help the hero rid himself of his flaw. Remember, though, to the hero it isn't a flaw at all; it is a defense against the dangers of life.

Thus, we already have a built-in conflict between the hero who wants to keep his flaw, and the ally whose only function is to rip that flaw right out of the hero's hot little hands. And, by the way, this is usually the most interesting conflict in the story.

The ally doesn't always succeed in his job, of course. For example, *Leaving Las Vegas* is a modern tragedy in the tradition of classical tragedies like *Oedipus Rex* and *Macbeth*. *Leaving Las Vegas* is about Ben (played by Nicholas Cage), a failed screenwriter who has come to Vegas to drink himself to death. The ally is Sera, Elizabeth Shue's character. As the ally, Sera's job is to prevent Ben from killing himself by giving him something to live for. Not to spoil the film for those of you who haven't seen it yet, but...Ben does drink himself to death. Sera fails in her job as an ally.

Another modern tragedy is the controversial love story *Brokeback Mountain*. As in many love stories, the opponent and the ally are the same person. Ennis is the hero of the story, and Jack is the opponent/ally. The job of the ally (Jack) is to help the hero (Ennis) to overcome his flaw. What is Ennis's flaw? Fear. Ennis's father took nine-year-old Ennis and his brother to see the fatally beaten body of a gay man, the implication being clear: This is what happens to those who step outside the sexual (and other kinds of) norm. Ennis will never be able to realize his romantic dreams because he believes (and perhaps correctly, given the time and place) that revealing his true sexual identity and living openly with his lover, Jack, means certain death.

Jack is not able to help Ennis overcome his fear. In fact, Jack himself validates Ennis's flaw by falling victim to exactly the kind of hatred that Ennis is afraid of. Nevertheless, even in failing to help the hero emerge triumphant, Jack is a heroic figure, because at least he tries, risking and losing his life in an attempt to find his place in the world as a gay man.

Many believe that the Oscar-winning *Million Dollar Baby* is a tragedy because of its tragic ending. However, despite the ending, the ally, Maggie, does her job: She helps Frankie overcome his flaw (fear of intimacy). Maggie not only gets Frankie to open up to her, but to perform an act that represents the ultimate in fatherly intimacy, love, and sacrifice. If he wasn't there for his own daughter, he was certainly there for Maggie.

Forrest Gump also has a tragic ending. There is a twist in this film, however. The authors made an interesting choice: They chose Forrest as the hero, but gave the flaw to his ally, Jenny. Her flaw is an inability to trust men, the result of brutal abuse she suffered as a child from her father. Therefore, Forrest actually has the ally's job, helping Jenny to overcome her mistrust of men and, more specifically, *him*. By remaining such a good man, Forrest succeeds in gaining Jenny's trust. He never does anything to threaten Jenny, including trying to force her to stay with him, even though he dies inside every time she leaves.

HOW MUCH TIME DOES THE HERO SPEND WITH THE ALLY?

In *Lethal Weapon*, Murtaugh (Danny Glover's character) is the hero's ally and stays by Riggs (Mel Gibson's character) throughout, helping him overcome his suicidal tendencies.

In *Wedding Crashers*, John (Owen Wilson's character) is the hero and Jeremy (Vince Vaughn's character) is the ally. Sure enough, John spends more time onscreen with Jeremy in the second act than with any other character.

Interestingly, when you take the script for *Wedding Crashers* and do a global search for the names "John," "Jeremy," and "Claire," you get telling results. John shows up more than 600 times. And Jeremy shows up more than 550 times. What about "Claire," John's opponent and love interest? Barely 100 times.

John and Jeremy, hero and ally, appear together on screen far more than John appears with Claire. In fact, even if you consider Claire's fiancé "Sack" as the real opponent, he only shows up 146 times.

In *Back to the Future*, the hero, Marty, shows up 339 times. Doc, the ally, appears 201 times. Biff, the opponent, shows up 64 times.

In *Lethal Weapon*, the hero Riggs (Mel Gibson's character) shows up 660 times, and his ally Murtaugh (Danny Glover's character) shows up 594 times. The opponent, Mr. Joshua (Gary Busey's character) shows up 142 times.

Does it always break down this neatly? No. In *As Good as it Gets*, one of the all-time great films, Jack Nicholson's character, Melvin, shows up 518 times. Carol, the love interest played by Helen Hunt, shows up 390 times. Simon, played brilliantly by Greg Kinnear, shows up 284 times. Despite this, I believe that Simon is the ally, and Carol is the opponent. It is Carol with whom Jack vies in the third and final act, and it is she who he "conquers" in the end.

Still, more often than not, the ally will spend more time on screen with the hero than the opponent does.

The Ally Suggests a Course of Action

Part of the ally's job is to suggest a course of action, either directly or as a result of the ally's own behavior. The method by which the ally helps the hero is called the ally's M.O. (modus operandi, method of operation). This can be through positive example, negative example, acting as a wise counselor, or other means.

In *Rocky*, Talia Shire's character Adrianna changes her own life, which inspires Rocky to believe he might be able to change his life for the better as well. She changes for the better by standing up to her tyrant brother Paulie and helps Rocky to realize that this kind of change is possible for him too. She never tells Rocky to change; she only leads by example and by being a positive role model. Again, the hero's ally has an M.O., a way of operating, a way of influencing the hero: by positive examples or by inspiration.

Or, the hero's ally might influence the hero by providing a *negative* role model. The hero's ally might have the same flaw as the hero, but is perhaps at an even lower level in his or her life because of that flaw. This allows the hero to see where he himself will someday be if he cannot overcome his own flaw.

The hero's ally might be a mentor or father figure who actively gives the hero advice. *Good Will Hunting* is a great example of this. Robin Williams' character Sean (the psychiatrist) is the father figure that Will Hunting (Matt Damon's character) needs.

In some stories, of course, the hero does not overcome his flaw, and he perishes in some way. This is usually because the ally was not strong enough or "right" enough to help the hero overcome his flaw. For example, in *Leaving Las Vegas*, Ben, a failed screenwriter, meets Sera, a prostitute. Her job as the ally is to save him. She fails, though, because she had not yet overcome her own flaws, and for that reason, was not strong enough to help Ben.

EXAMPLES FROM FAMOUS FILMS

In *Million Dollar Baby*, Morgan Freeman's character Scrap suggests a course of action for Frankie simply by beginning

---

to help Maggie in her training. Eventually Frankie takes over Maggie's training himself, but Scrap starts the ball moving, suggesting the course of action by setting an example for the hero.

In *Hook*, Tinker Bell suggests a course of action for Peter, namely returning to Neverland and becoming Peter Pan again in order to rescue his kids from Captain Hook.

In *Brokeback Mountain*, Jack (the ally) suggests that he and Ennis buy a ranch and live and work together as lovers.

In *Batman Begins*, the villain Henri Ducard comes to Bruce Wayne's aid in the Himalayas, becoming his ally. Ducard teaches him martial arts and philosophy, shaping him and making him strong. But in the end, this ally is a negative role model—he shows Bruce Wayne what happens when power is used wrongly. He shows what Bruce might have become if he had taken the wrong road, the road Ducard himself took.

OUR STORY

Our ally should be someone who can believably help Ross overcome his flaw. Well, why don't we make this simple and clean—Ross's ally is someone right there in his workplace, someone he has fallen in love with, even though his flaw keeps him from having an actual relationship with her.

Our ally is a woman he works with. To help our hero, she'll have to be a strong person, so why not make her the company owner? Let's call her Leslie.

Who is Leslie? Well, as mentioned, she'll be strong, which oftentimes brings its own problems for a woman in a misogynistic society. Does being strong make her give up some of her so-called "femininity"? Did she inherit the business from her father? That's too easy and makes her too weak to really help Ross.

All right, then, let's make it that Leslie inherited the business from her *mother*. That's a nice way of going against type, of thumbing our nose at sexist stereotypes. More importantly, however, it's believable that she's strong enough to help Ross, because she was taught strength by her mother.

6.

The Life-Changing Event

The life-changing event usually occurs at the end of Act One. It is usually instigated by the opponent, which forces the hero to respond and change his life in some way related to his flaw. This life-changing event always carries with it a challenge, threat or opportunity. In a tragedy such as *Leaving Las Vegas* or *Brokeback Mountain*, the hero fails to meet, overcome, or choose the life-changing event, and in some way perishes—physically as in *Leaving Las Vegas* or spiritually/emotionally as in *Brokeback Mountain*.

The life-changing event should force the hero to choose between his flaw and an opportunity presented by the life-changing event. This is one of the most important statements you'll read in this book. By making the hero choose between his flaw and an opportunity, the life-changing event increases the cost of having that flaw.

For example, in *Hook*, Peter's flaw deprives him of his inner child and whatever joy and freedom comes with that

---

inner child. After Captain Hook kidnaps Peter's children, Peter's flaw keeps him from having his actual, real-life children. Do you see how the life-changing event has suddenly increased the cost of having this flaw?

In *Leaving Las Vegas*, Ben ends up dying, never even attempting to save himself. Still, there is a point in the story when he meets Sera, where he could have made a different choice. He could have chosen the love offered by Sera.

Instead, Ben chooses to keep his flaw, which is his suicidal determination to drink himself to death. So his flaw costs him not just his empty, failed life, but potentially a life with a beautiful and loving woman.

A story in which the hero chooses his flaw instead of some opportunity is called a tragedy, as in Greek or Shakespearean tragedy (e.g., *Oedipus Rex*, *Romeo and Juliet*, or *Macbeth*).

The relationship between the hero's character flaw and the life-changing event forms the heart of any well-written screenplay. More about this later, but let me reemphasize: The relationship between the hero's flaw and the life-changing event is the most important element in any well-written story.

Note also that in every example I give below, the opponent instigates the life-changing event. This, too, is an important technique to remember.

EXAMPLES FROM FAMOUS FILMS

In *Batman Begins*, the life-changing event is Ducard taking Bruce Wayne out of prison and up to the monastery high in the Himalayas to train him. This presents a great challenge to Bruce to make something worthwhile out of his life despite the guilt he feels for his perceived part in his parents' death.

In *Million Dollar Baby*, the life-changing event is the arrival of the female boxer, Maggie, into Frankie's life, wearing him down until he finally agrees to train her. The reason this is such a risk for Frankie is that he lost his own daughter for some reason we don't know—she's still alive, probably, but won't answer any of his letters, and it eats at him. Now he risks becoming emotionally involved with a young woman perhaps his daughter's age. The pain caused by his failure with his daughter makes this new relationship incredibly risky.

In *Hook*, when Captain Hook kidnaps Peter's children, the challenges, risks, and opportunities are obvious.

In *Rocky*, the life-changing event is Apollo Creed offering Rocky a chance at the world championship. Even though Rocky believes himself to be a loser, the magnitude of the opportunity is too great to refuse—even for him. He has to respond, and in the process of responding begins to overcome his flaw and redefine himself as someone strong and courageous enough to "go the distance."

OUR STORY

If the life-changing event is something that forces the hero to make a choice between his flaw and some opportunity, then it's going to have to be an event that presents an opportunity he can't refuse (like Rocky fighting for the world championship) or a threat he can't ignore (like Peter's kids being kidnapped by Captain Hook).

We have unlimited latitude here, but let's continue to keep it simple. If Ross has the hots for the ally Leslie, then let's put Leslie in danger from the opponent, Matt. This might force Ross to choose between his cowardice and the chance to save Leslie—the woman he loves.

We may change this later, but let's say that Matt is embezzling funds from the company, which threatens the very existence of the business. Now remember—this is not just a business that Leslie has put her blood, sweat, and tears into; it's a business that belonged to her late mother. The threat of losing this business is a big one.

In addition, when a business goes bankrupt, everyone in the company is affected—people lose their jobs and maybe their pensions. Older employees face the fact that they may not be able to get another job. If Leslie is as nice as I think she is, losing both her mother's company and her cherished employees would be a pretty big hit.

Let's make sure we keep one thing in mind as well: Matt is not just crooked, he's *dangerous*.

So…what decision does Ross face now? Well, he can just walk away and find another set of enabling circumstances that will allow him to continue being a meek little accountant. That would, however, cost him any chance he has at being with Leslie. It would also haunt him because he'd be walking away from all the people he has worked with and come to like.

Ross has to decide between the safety of his flaw and the opportunity (and danger) of love and friendship. Again, we'll build on this later.

7. JEOPaRDY

The hero must have something to lose—either physically or emotionally. If there is no conflict, jeopardy, or high stakes, there is no interest, excitement, or tension in the story, and people will not be drawn into it.

Things *cannot* come easily to your hero—he has to pay a price to get what he wants. The ultimate price is to give up his flaw, because he sees it as protection against the cruelty of life.

Asking a hero to give up his flaw should be like asking someone to take off his bulletproof vest in the middle of a gun battle. This is why the life-changing event must be *believably* strong enough to force the hero to choose between his flaw and the opportunity, threat, or challenge offered by the life-changing event.

EXAMPLES FROM FAMOUS FILMS

In *Brokeback Mountain*, Ennis has everything to lose. Wyoming during 1963 was not a safe place to be gay, so he's certain that he risks death by being who he is. Just as important, perhaps, he stands to lose his family, friends, job. This works well to pull us into his world, to feel the fear that he feels. The audience understands why he chooses his flaw over his opportunity, no matter how badly it hurts them to watch him self-destruct.

In *Batman Begins*, Bruce Wayne faces tremendous jeopardy. First, there is the physical jeopardy of being killed by his enemy Ducard. Then there's the jeopardy of Ducard destroying the city which Bruce's parents did so much to build and preserve. There's also the emotional jeopardy—Bruce feels responsible for his parents' death, and protecting Gotham is his way of making up for it. If he fails to protect Gotham from Ducard, he fails to honor his parents' memory and fails to redeem himself.

OUR STORY

We have already described the decision that Ross has to make: He has to choose between losing a chance at a relationship with Leslie (and the friends he has among the company employees) on the one hand, and losing the personal security his flaw provides him on the other.

What, however, is the *specific* jeopardy he faces? Well, if he chooses to keep his flaw, he loses Leslie, his co-workers, and his job, not to mention being forever burdened by the knowledge (and shame) that he abandoned Leslie and his workmates in their hour of need.

On the other hand, if Ross decides to try to overcome his flaw to help Leslie and his co-workers, he must face Matt and whatever Matt can do to him. Since we want drama and action and tension in this story, we'll simply make Matt someone dangerous, someone who would quite believably hurt anyone who got in his way.

The biggest jeopardy of all for Ross, however, is repeating the disaster of years before, when his cowardice got people killed.

8. COMBINING STORY ELEMENTS

You now know that you need a hero, an opponent, an ally, and the other essential elements. What you may not know is which hero you need, which ally would be appropriate, which opponent would be a believable and interesting foil for your hero, and so on.

The good news is that you only need to know one or two of the necessary story elements in order to figure out all the rest. If you figure out who your hero should be (priest undergoing a crisis in faith; a boy who finds a space alien in his closet), you can use that one story element (the hero) to figure out all the other story elements you need for your screenplay.

Even better news, the process of finding out the various elements is a simple one. It's the process that underlies all of screenwriting: asking and answering questions.

For instance, let's start out by picking only one element and then going through the process of figuring out what the other elements in our story should be. This is similar to what we have been doing in building our story, but this time we'll start with a different story element.

USING ONE ELEMENT TO FIGURE OUT OTHERS

Let's assume that we are beginning with an interesting life-changing event and use it to figure out what the other six essential elements of our story can be.

Let's say that the life-changing event in this instance is a young woman who wins a huge lottery. Now you, the screenwriter, must ask questions to figure out what the other elements are.

What opportunity does this life-changing event offer? The chance to be wealthy, of course. If our hero is *already* wealthy, the lottery really doesn't offer much of an opportunity. The full effect of the lottery comes only if our hero is hurting for money, or at least not already wealthy. Now, if our hero is poor, and the lottery solves that problem, the script is over by page thirty: A poor young woman wins a lottery and lives happily ever after.

So, if our hero *is* poor, and the lottery would prevent her from being poor, the character flaw must be something that makes our hero *choose* to be poor. Winning the lottery would force our hero to choose between her flaw and the opportunity presented by the life-changing event of winning a lottery.

What flaw in our hero would make it undesirable, difficult, or even impossible to take advantage of the opportunity presented by the life-changing event? Maybe she's anti-materialistic. She might be a nun or other type of ascetic with a vow of poverty. Or, again, maybe she's from a rich family whose corruption has driven her to renounce wealth. Or maybe she has so many friends in her lower-class lifestyle that she's afraid of losing them if she accepts the lottery money and the attendant inevitable change in lifestyle.

Or maybe her lover is a poor but hardworking man, and she knows his pride would never accept being a "kept man" if she suddenly became wealthy. We've seen this story repeatedly among wealthy celebrities who marry "ordinary" people. Think of Britney Spears marrying a lowly dancer, and Liz Taylor marrying the infamous "bagel boy."

Okay, we could go a number of ways here, so let me add just one of a myriad of storylines based on the only element we have to work with—the life-changing event.

Maybe the lottery isn't an actual lottery, but rather an unexpected windfall that results from the hero's efforts. Let's say that our hero is a writer or other type of artist who finally makes it big with a book, screenplay, song, or whatever, and the windfall is huge, perhaps accompanied by fame and status.

This woman has been striving for years to "make it," and she met and fell in love with her lover when neither of them was successful. Now she alone has made it, and the stresses on all her relationships will yield strong and believable drama and conflict.

If the hero is middle-class or even lower-class, a woman who struggles with bills but also enjoys the very unsophisticated pleasures of life with other people of her social and economic class, this windfall will cause a rift between the newly rich-and-famous hero and the working-class people she loves and lives among.

Let's go a step further here and create some more of the crucial elements. First, for the flaw, we have many choices, but let's arbitrarily go with the hero having a fear of rising above her present station.

Okay, but then who's the opponent? The lover, I would guess. Why is he the opponent? Because he opposes either the hero's desire to avoid success (which would also make him her ally), or he opposes the hero's success itself (if he does not have her best interest at heart but is acting out of jealousy, for instance).

The most important question we can ask in order to determine whether an opponent is "right" for the part is: Does he instigate the life-changing event? Let's say that the opponent, the hero's lover, submits one of her works of art (painting, song, novel, screenplay) to a publisher or producer or gallery owner, which is what leads to the sudden success and financial windfall.

Who's the hero's ally? If the lover does decide to oppose the hero's success, a neighbor or friend of the same economic class would make an excellent foil. She might be someone who understands the hero's fear, but who is also best suited to helping her overcome it because she understands the pain and frustration of being poor and insecure.

So, now we have a hero, life-changing event, opponent, character flaw, and hero's ally, just from knowing one element—the life-changing event. I could (and might!) go on to develop this story further, but even as it is now, it serves as an excellent example of how we can go from one element to a full story description in a short period of time, just by using the relationships between the elements of storytelling structure.

However, don't be afraid to alter any element if it makes it easier to write the best possible story.

Another Option

My switching the life-changing event from a lottery to an earned reward made this story work much more easily. Whatever works, do it. Often, it is not what you think it should be—go with the flow, as long as it is helping you say what you want to say and helping you create an interesting, powerful story.

But let's say you really wanted our hero to win the lottery, and you feel like that would be the most successful way to tell the story. It's important to think about what problems we face with this storyline. Well, if the life-changing event is the completely fortuitous event of winning a lottery, how can that event be instigated by the opponent?

Let's say that the hero comes from a wealthy family. It's a family that has abused that wealth and cheated others to get it, keep it, and increase it. The members of the family are so obsessed with wealth that they have ignored their own daughter—our hero.

So now we have two elements—the lottery win and a hero who is anti-materialistic because of her upbringing. Now I don't mean to make anti-materialism the hero's flaw, because it is not in itself a flaw. In fact, anti-materialism might be seen as a spiritually enlightened point of view. So we use the term to help define the hero, not as a character flaw. We also have an opponent—either one of the parents will do, but let's say it's the father.

Not bad. We have several of the seven essential elements, but one of the elements, the opponent, is missing something important: He, the father, is not the instigator of the life-changing event. But we can fix that, using our storytelling tools—and a little imagination and ingenuity.

Let's say that the father is constantly trying to make his estranged daughter "see the light" and come back into the materialistic upper class. He visits his daughter just before the life-changing event to try to bring her back into that fold. They argue, and the angry father throws a lottery ticket onto our hero's coffee table, saying: "Here, I bought this on the way over as a peace offering, but I guess it's gone too far for that now. Why don't you think of it as representing your life in this rat-hole of yours: All the odds stacked against you."

The father leaves, and the daughter angrily balls up the lottery ticket and throws it into a corner. Then, days later, she discovers that the ticket is the winning ticket in a huge, multi-million dollar lottery. So now we have an opponent-caused life-changing event that is going to force our anti-materialistic hero to choose between her principles (and bitter memories of her family's materialism) and a ten-million-dollar jackpot.

We need at least one more thing: a character flaw. Let's say that our hero's flaw is her fear of becoming like her parents if she has their kind of money—falling prey to greed, cruelty, and crass materialism. It is, more specifically, a lack of faith in her own good intentions that keeps her locked in poverty and failure as a way to avoid the kind of temptations to which her own parents fell victim.

In a way, this is like *Oedipus Rex*, the classic Greek tragedy. Oedipus goes to a fortuneteller who tells him that he will kill his father and marry his mother. Believing that this is actually within his capability, he flees his city. Unknown to Oedipus, he was adopted as a child. And guess where he ends up? Right, with his biological family in his home city. There, not knowing that he is now with his "real" family, he kills his father and marries his mother. When he finds out, he puts his own eyes out.

What was Oedipus' flaw? His failure to believe in his own goodness. If he had believed in himself, he would not have fled his home and his adopted family, and he would have relied on his innate sense of goodness. He would have avoided the predicted tragedy.

The hero of our story is a little like that. She eschews wealth because she does not believe she is good enough to have wealth without abusing it the way her parents have done.

So now we've got a hero, a life-changing event, a flaw, and an opponent. How about an ally for our hero? Let's go with her lover from the last scenario—a good-hearted, hard-working man who can never seem to make it above middle-class or lower-middle-class despite his intentions and good character. Suddenly his lover, our hero, is potentially a multi-multi-millionaire. What does that do to their relationship? Moreover, what does it do to our hero's fear that wealth will spoil her life the way it has her parents'?

Since the lover is the hero's ally and his job is to help the hero overcome her flaw, this earnest but unsuccessful young man must be able to offer her something. He has to have some way of influencing her in a way that will help her overcome her flaw. It could be as a positive role model who is comfortable either with or without money because he knows who he really is; he's centered enough to handle both situations without becoming either despondent or arrogant. It could also be as a negative role model. Maybe he becomes so obsessed with the money that our hero is convinced that the money will destroy her life just as it destroyed her parents' lives. Alternatively, maybe she sees that she is not like the ally and does not have to fear the corruption of money.

Either way would make an interesting story, depending on another question: How do you want your hero to end up at the conclusion of the story? Do you want her to be rich and able to handle those riches? Or do you want her to be poor but able to appreciate what she has without feeling compelled to have her parents' kind of wealth and all of its danger?

By knowing a single element in your story, you can build on it to create the other elements, followed by a logline (a short description of your story, including all seven essential elements; see Chapter 14), an outline or treatment (a short description of every scene in the script; see Chapter 15), then finally the story itself, all based on one single element. It could be the hero, flaw, life-changing event, opponent, theme (what the story is really about, e.g., greed, self-esteem, hatred, violence, love, family), hero's ally, ally's M.O., enabling circumstances, and so forth.

THE HERO'S DESIRE

A reminder: The hero's goal or desire at the beginning of the script is not always a goal that would benefit the hero. For instance, a miser's desire might be to hold onto his money. The opponent might be a loving, generous person who wants the miser/hero to give his money to a worthwhile cause. If the hero's miserliness causes him to be lonely, unhappy, mistrustful, and unable to enjoy his wealth, then the opponent is actually doing the hero a favor by preventing him from achieving his desire, which is to continue being miserly at the cost of his own happiness. This is one of the classic situations where the opponent is also the ally—someone that prevents the hero from getting what he wants, but also forces him to eliminate his flaw.

STAYING WITHIN THE CHARACTER'S ABILITIES

It must be within the hero's physical power to change his flaw. If he can't play Carnegie Hall because he lost his hands in an accident, it's not a character flaw. It's a physical flaw, and there's not a hell of a lot he can do about it.

On the other hand, the real flaw might be that this physically handicapped former pianist has given up on life. There *is* something he can do about that: He can train a protégé to play in his place, and/or write a piece of music that someone else can play. There is still a triumph to be achieved—or, possibly, a failure, if the hero decides instead to wallow in his own self-pity.

THE RELATIONSHIP BETWEEN THE CHARACTER
FLAW AND THE LIFE-CHANGING EVENT

I'll be coming back to this point over and over again because of its importance: The life-changing event must force your main character to choose between his flaw and an opportunity presented by the life-changing event.

Conversely, your main character's flaw must stand in the way of him successfully responding to the life-changing event. Otherwise, he can respond to the event without having to change. And if he can avoid changing, he will. If he does not change, there is no story. This relationship between the hero's character flaw and the life-changing event is perhaps the most important relationship in the script. This relationship exists in all well-made films, especially in dark tragedies such as *Leaving Las Vegas*.

In *Leaving Las Vegas*, Ben's character flaw is his suicidal despair. The life-changing event is that he meets Sera. Sera represents life, and Ben is forced to choose between death and life. Because it's a tragedy, Ben chooses death. However, by looking at the elements of the movie, a screenwriter can easily envision several endings. All of those endings are based on the relationship between the character flaw and the life-changing event.

THe STRUCTURE

2

9.

PROLOGUE

Now we're going to investigate some of the elements of structure in a story. The prologue consists of what happens before the screenplay gets started, also known as the backstory. The backstory consists of those events that create the hero's flaw, his opinion of himself, and his primary state of mind at the beginning of the story. The reason this is important to know is that it makes the hero's flaw logical, and it will help the writer to determine what the hero needs to do to overcome that flaw.

THE ULTIMATE LIST OF STRUCTURAL ELEMENTS

This outline is a brief overview of what we will be discussing in the next few chapters.

Major Backstory Elements:

- Point of Origin
- Original Circumstance

- Original Challenge
- Original Defining Decision
- Original Self-Definition
- Primary Emotional State
- Character Flaw

Major Elements of the First Act

- The Hero and His Flaw
- The Hero's Redeeming Qualities
- The Hero's Enabling Circumstances
- The Hero's Motivation and Point of View
- The Opponent and the Hero's Ally
- The Life-Changing Event

Major Elements of the First Part of the Second Act

- The Objective and Subjective Storylines
- The Ticking Clock
- Hero's Emotional Reaction to the Life-Changing Event
- Hero's Physical Reaction to the Life-Changing Event
- Hero's Ally Offers Help
- Hero Determines the Course of Action
- Hero and Hero's Ally Instigate the First Action Against the Opponent
- Opponent Counterattacks and States His Point of View
- Ally Confronts Hero About Balk
- Hero Renews His Determination to Meet the Life-Changing Event
- Hero Expands His Area of Concern
- Hero Confronts His Character Flaw
- Hero Convinces Ally to Give Him Another Chance
- Hero Proves Himself to Ally

- Hero Partially Redeems Himself, Bonds With Ally
- Second Act Confrontation Between Hero and Ally
- Hero Reveals Part of His Character Flaw to Ally
- Ally Makes Demand of Hero
- Ally Reveals Own Struggles

Major Elements of the Second Part of the Second Act

- Hero's Choice
- Hero and Ally Unite Against Opponent
- Hero Expands His Area of Concern Wider
- The Opponent Counters Hero and Ally, the Unraveling
- Opponent Increases Area of Threat
- Hero Breaks His Own Rules
- Opponent Performs Act Forcing Hero to Completely Abandon His Flaw
- Hero Learns True Danger
- Second Circumstance, Challenge, Decision, Self-Definition, and Emotional State
- Final Expansion of Hero's Area of Concern
- The Point of No Return

Major Elements of the Third Act

- All or Nothing
- Damage to Hero Mounts
- The Low Point
- Hero Discovers Way to Fight Back
- The Audience Discovers Full Extent of Opponent's Threat
- Hero Learns of Increased Threat
- The Final Battle

- Hero Fully Engages Opponent
- Hero Restates Point of View
- Hero Defeats or is Defeated by Opponent
- Hero, Changed by Events in the Story, Faces the Future
- Optional Final Twist

Now let's define some key terms.

The **point of origin** is first in a sequence of events that leads to the hero developing or adopting his flaw. It is when the hero is thrown into some circumstance.

The **original circumstance** is the circumstance into which the hero is thrown. War, abuse, marriage, divorce, widowhood, fame, infamy...

The **original challenge** is asked or demanded of the hero. It is a challenge he has to meet whether he's prepared for it or not.

The **original defining decision** and **original self-definition** is the decision the hero makes in reaction to the original challenge. As a result of this decision, the hero will define himself in some way, perhaps as a loser or a winner.

The **primary emotional state** of the hero arises from the original decision and original self-definition: anger, hatred, fear, shame, and so forth.

The **character flaw** is the overt expression of the emotional state. Will the hero turn inward with his hatred and let it eat him up? Or will he turn outward and become a terrorist or murderer, or just a selfish, unpleasant person driven by his hatred to succeed at other people's expense?

BACKSTORY VERSUS RUNNING START

Backstory consists of those events leading up to the beginning of the movie. The beginning of the movie is the point in the hero's life at which we drop in.

You can show the audience your hero's backstory in just about any way that's effective. For example, let's look at *Forrest Gump* and *Million Dollar Baby*. *Forrest Gump* begins with Forrest as a child, and we actually watch him grow up to become the person he is for the rest of the movie.

In *Million Dollar Baby*, we begin with Frankie exhibiting the flaw that holds him back, but we don't immediately see how he got to this point in his life. We eventually learn that he feels responsible for the loss of Scrap's eye, and for whatever drove a wedge between Frankie and his estranged daughter. This is called a "running start."

The amount of backstory you show can vary greatly. In *Forrest Gump*, we see it all on screen. In *Rocky*, we see one short shot of a photo in Rocky Balboa's apartment, and then one reference to Rocky's past when he says, about halfway through the movie, that his "old man" had told him: "…I weren't born with much brain so I better use my body." This is the motivation for everything we see in Rocky—his lifestyle, his failure, his attitude toward being a loser.

Most films use the "running start" approach, but it's up to you because you're the writer, and it's your script. I prefer the approach of beginning a film with the hero already exhibiting the character flaw, because then we have the joy of discovering who the hero is and why he is the way he is.

EXAMPLES FROM FAMOUS FILMS

Brokeback Mountain follows our model fairly closely.

Though the film starts *in media res*, the audience quickly learns of Ennis's childhood. After being raised in the racist, sexist South, Ennis gets society's message loud and clear: He is undesirable, perverted, and deserves to be killed. The original challenge is for Ennis to find a way to physically survive while remaining true to who he is. He manages the physical survival, but he loses himself and his courage.

The decision he makes, or the original defining decision, is to hide who he is. The self-definition, as stated above, is that he's undesirable, perverted, something to be killed. The primary emotional state that arises is fear—fear of being found out, of being killed like the murdered gay man from his youth.

Ennis' flaw is his inability to commit to Jack, or even to reveal who he is. Because this film is a tragedy, Ennis is unable to overcome his fear, and he rejects Jack's offer to live their lives together on their own ranch.

OUR STORY

Let's go back to the story we started in Part 1 and begin adding the structural elements. We know that our hero Ross is a coward at the beginning, so we need to invent a backstory that could have believably caused him to become the coward he is. Now, although in earlier chapters we said that Ross was a former Green Beret, let's start this section with just the idea that Ross is a coward, and then progress to the point where we determine he is a Green Beret.

What past event was so traumatic that it shaped Ross for years to come? Well, how about we begin with a guy who's going to war? War is a fertile ground for conflict and drama. Some of the greatest movies have been war movies, such as *The Sands of Iwo Jima*, *Full Metal Jacket*, *Coming Home*, *Schindler's List*, *Sophie's Choice*, *Casablanca*, *The Great Escape*, and *The Killing Fields*.

So Ross is a soldier. This becomes the point of origin for our story. Ross is sent to war. The original circumstance then becomes the war itself. To make it a little more complicated, let's say that Ross does not agree politically with this war, but he believes in his duty to serve.

Now, during the war, Ross is asked to risk his life to attack the enemy in some form—this is the original challenge.

The Original Defining Decision and the Original Self-Definition

Ross now has a choice between fight and flight. Ross decides to flee, but not because of his complicated political views--purely because of fear. This is the original defining decision. We call it that because it is the decision that will lead to Ross defining himself—and/or being defined *by* others. The original self-definition is the definition Ross thereafter applies to himself.

Since Ross' original defining decision was to flee out of fear instead of principle, his original self-definition is that of a coward.

The Primary Emotional State

Ross' original self-definition of himself as a coward creates in him a primary emotional state. This could be resentment toward his government for putting him in a position that he did not feel he was capable of handling. Or, Ross' primary emotional state could be fear that someone will discover his cowardice, or perhaps fear that he will be put in a position to repeat his "cowardice." It could be guilt or self-loathing. Let's pick fear. So Ross has a fear of his own fear.

The Character Flaw

Ross' emotional state will express itself overtly as a behavior of some sort. If Ross feels guilt, he may develop an exaggerated desire to please others in an attempt to expiate those feelings of guilt.

If Ross feels ashamed of his original defining decision, he may push people away for fear of someone finding out about his past.

If Ross is bitter toward the government for having placed him in a situation where he was eventually embarrassed by his conduct, he may act bitterly toward the world as a whole, even if it was his decision to go in the first place. (Another facet of his cowardice may be blaming others for his fears and problems.)

Ross, as a coward, may feel unworthy of having happiness or love or friendship. He may go into denial, and he may lie, claiming to be a war hero, and perhaps build an entire life on this lie.

There are many possible scenarios for our cowardly hero Ross. This is important to know, because if there was only one choice open to you based on the original defining decision, you as a writer would be hamstrung.

This overt expression of the primary emotional state is the hero's character flaw. For our story, let's have Ross push people away, for fear they'll discover who he really is. By pushing people away, he guarantees his privacy, but he also ensures that he is a lonely man—by choice, but no less lonely for it being voluntary.

This is an interesting plot line because there is always something fascinating about a man who is a trained killer, but who also exhibits qualities of cowardice.

The contradiction carries with it an innate conflict between the two sides of Ross' nature. This hook could make this a high-concept piece: "A cowardly Green Beret takes on a deadly terrorist in an attempt to overcome his cowardice and regain his self-respect."

10. ACT ONE

In a three-act structure, the first act ends with the life-changing event, around page thirty or so. The next act shows a confrontation and reflects how the hero decides either to overcome or embrace his flaw, and the third act shows the hero and opponent battling and emerges with a victory. For the purposes of this book, however, we are breaking the three-act structure into four parts, which means the second act is composed of two thirty-page sections. This technique means that in the first part of the second act, the character will face a conflict that forces him to choose between the comfort of his flaw and what he knows to be right, and the second part of the second act will show the hero and the opponent battling.

While the first act has traditionally been about thirty pages long, of late there is a trend toward shorter scripts, and the first act now tends to be closer to twenty-five pages long. It has been suggested that the trend toward shorter scripts is meant to allow distributors to give an extra showing per day, especially of mediocre big-budget films that need to be shown as often as possible in as short a time as possible, before word-of-mouth kills them. I'd hate to think that this is actually true, but given the lack of quality in most Hollywood films, perhaps it is believable that distributors would resort to these kinds of tactics.

Introduce the Hero and His Flaw

The purpose of the first act of your screenplay is to describe and define the hero of the story.

First and foremost, this means showing the one, deep-seated character flaw that keeps your hero from being all that he can be. We know that in real life we are all rife with flaws (at least that's what my ex-wives always insisted). However, in the course of a two-hour motion picture, we don't have time to deal with a hero who has a dozen flaws, all of which have to be resolved or at least addressed and explored.

For that reason, screenwriters must focus on one flaw that most severely impacts the hero, and those around him, at the beginning of the story.

This flaw can be fear, bitterness, meekness, co-dependency, greed—anything that is serious enough to hinder your hero and deep-seated enough to be very difficult for the hero to overcome. It also has to be something that at one time served as a way of coping with some kind of trauma.

In *As Good as it Gets*, we see Melvin Udall and his flaw quite early. The first scene shows him throwing the neighbor's dog down the trash chute, showing that he's antisocial.

It is expressed in a number of ways, but the main point is that what this guy needs to learn is how to get along with others—neighbors, dogs, waitresses, the world as a whole. We can also see how his antisocial behavior serves him. He has so many phobias—germs, going out of his apartment, homophobia, people breaking into his apartment, stepping on cracks, panic attacks—that keeping people at bay must seem like the only way of coping with the endless threats in the world.

In *The Verdict*, we start with Paul Newman's character Frank Galvin handing out business cards at a funeral home—he's a lawyer and quite literally an ambulance chaser. He's down-and-out and has given up all attempts at self-respectability. We'll learn later why he's the way he is, but we get it loud and clear: This is one big loser. We learn later that he once handled a case that went terribly bad, and he sold out in some way. His drunkenness is his way of making sure it will never happen again. Who will trust him with that kind of case again, since he's such a loser? You see, even the worst flaw can have some kind of payoff to the person who owns that flaw. In fact, in order for them to maintain such a flaw, it must have *significant* payoff.

In the first draft of *Wedding Crashers*, as we discussed earlier, Jeremy tells a client, "Marriage is a curse. It's our punishment for original sin." He then goes into John's office and they plan their wedding season, which consists of crashing weddings and taking the vulnerable women to bed before fleeing the scene. It is clear that both of these men have somehow been hurt, and hurt badly, by women. Their protection is to be lifelong bachelors, going from one one-night stand to another, crashing weddings as a way of negating the value of both weddings and women.

However you do it, the first act is where you introduce your hero and his flaw.

Show the Hero's Redeeming Qualities

In addition to the character flaw, the first act is used to show your hero's redeeming qualities. These are qualities that mitigate the hero's character flaw and make the hero either interesting and/or likable enough for us to spend two hours and ten bucks watching him try to make his way to the end of his journey.

Let's go back to *The Verdict*. Paul Newman's character Frank gets thrown out of the funeral home when he tries to hand his card to the recently deceased's widow. He lands on his ass on the sidewalk, scrambles to his feet, and then does something important as he wipes himself off. He glances around, embarrassed, looking for anyone who saw him being thrown out into the street. It's just enough to keep the chance for redemption open—he knows how far he's fallen, and he's still capable of being embarrassed about it. It's the redeeming qualities of the hero that makes the rest of the story possible and that keep us in the theater to follow this putz to the end of the story.

Never underestimate the importance of the redeeming qualities of your hero. Without them, you lose the audience right off the bat because they will not cheer for an irredeemable character.

Show the Hero's Enabling Circumstances

Remember, the enabling circumstance is the circumstance that your hero finds or creates that allows him to maintain his flaw. In *Million Dollar Baby* and *Rocky*, we're introduced to the enabling circumstances early in the first act. It's the fight game, the dirty, pragmatic, ultra-realistic world of boxing, where you always get knocked down and you always get back up, but you know that the next knockdown is coming so you don't even bother hoping for anything else. That's just the way life is, right?

This enabling circumstance allows Rocky and Frankie to keep on going, to be who they are without standing out— two men who've given up, one because of what his father told him, the other because of having failed in his duty as a father to his daughter. Frankie also failed Scrap by letting him finish a fight that resulted in Scrap losing an eye.

In *Good Will Hunting*, we see Will Hunting in the bars of South Boston with his street-wise friends, and in the halls of Massachusetts Institute of Technology where he works as a janitor. Both of these environments serve Will's purposes: He can be a stupid street kid despite the fact that he's a genius beyond compare, while also being near the greatest minds in the country at MIT. And he doesn't have to give up his flaw in either circumstance.

Show the Hero's Motivation and Point of View
One of the most important things to accomplish in the first act is to express the hero's motivation and point of view. A major part of the battle between the hero and opponent is the clash of their points of view. The hero's and opponent's points of view need to be clearly expressed. They can be expressed verbally and, even better, through their actions.

For instance, if you have a hero who believes strongly in doing his duty, and you have an opponent who believes that doing his duty has caused him nothing but harm, you have a fundamental clash between these two characters. This clash will add depth to the story as a whole.

Of course, you can also have both hero and opponent share the same motivation but have different points of view about how to *express* that motivation. For example, your hero might be a cop who fights for justice by upholding the law. On the other hand, maybe your opponent is a terrorist who fights for justice by trying to destroy what he sees as a corrupt government and unjust laws.

Introduce the Opponent and the Hero's Ally

In the first act, you should also introduce your opponent and *perhaps* the hero's ally. (Sometimes the hero's ally appears at the beginning of the second act, right after the life-changing event.)

The opponent will usually appear no later than the life-changing event because, after all, the opponent instigates that event.

In *Million Dollar Baby*, Maggie, the opponent, appears within the first five pages or so, but doesn't really instigate the life-changing event until about thirty pages later. Scrap, the ally, is introduced from the beginning as the narrator, and appears himself about ten pages into the script.

There's no formula for when you introduce your opponent and ally, except you'd be best served to do it somewhere within the first forty pages or so.

Remember, too, that there are really only three indispensable characters in a film—the hero, the hero's ally, and the opponent. Sometimes the same person is both the ally *and* the opponent, but the roles must be accounted for. The hero's ally spends the most time with the hero, especially in the second act. The hero's ally directly or indirectly helps the hero overcome his character flaw. For example, in *Lethal Weapon*, Riggs (Mel Gibson) is the hero, and Murtaugh (Danny Glover) is the hero's ally. Murtaugh helps Riggs overcome his character flaw, which is Riggs's desire to commit suicide.

I can hear the question already: "Can you have a screenplay with only two or maybe even only one character?" My answer is always the same—you can have any kind of screenplay you're talented enough to pull off. Take *Cast Away*, for example. It only had two characters that were consistently present, and it did well at the box office. Director Bob Zemeckis (*Forrest Gump* and *Back to the Future*) and writer William Broyles, Jr. (*Jarhead, Unfaithful, Apollo 13*) did a great job when you consider that there was essentially only Tom Hanks and a volleyball. But even here they cheated by having Helen Hunt lurking in the background in his memory and showing up at the beginning and end of the film. However, they pulled it off, at least financially. If you have the resources of a Zemeckis, the talent of a William Broyles, Jr., and two Oscar-winning actors (Hanks and Hunt) at your disposal, you might want to try that one-character script you've been meaning to write. Otherwise, you might want to try the formula used to write *Forrest Gump, Steel Magnolias, Good Will Hunting, As Good as It Gets, Casablanca*, and so on.

Introduce the Life-Changing Event

At the end of the first act, there is an event that is almost always instigated by the opponent. This event is a threat, a challenge, and/or an opportunity. The challenge is such that the hero cannot respond to it successfully unless he overcomes his character flaw. The challenge also happens to be so tempting, so hard to resist, that the hero can only resist it at his peril.

Sometimes the hero will accept the challenge and still lose, but in a sense the hero wins simply by accepting the challenge regardless of the outcome. *Rocky* is like that, which is why we all loved the movie so much and why it won an Oscar for best picture and was nominated for best screenplay. Although Rocky loses the boxing match, he wins by accepting the challenge fully and going the distance.

Often the hero will try to respond to the challenge without dropping his character flaw. Remember, to the hero, his flaw is the only way of surviving; it's his suit of armor. But regardless of how important the hero thinks his flaw is, he will eventually have to either abandon or overcome that flaw or else fail in his attempt to respond to the life-changing event. The reason the hero will try to maintain his flaw is that he does not view it as a flaw, but as a defense mechanism. So he will hold onto it for as long as he possibly can, even while trying to take advantage of the life-changing event.

In *Hook*, the grown-up Peter does not immediately revert to being Peter Pan upon learning that Captain Hook

"You make me want to be a better man."

—As Good as It Gets

"Mama always said life was like a box of chocolates. You never know what you're gonna' get."

—Forrest Gump

"If you build it, he will come."

—Field of Dreams

has kidnapped his children. He does not even revert to being Peter Pan when he is brought to Neverland by Tinkerbell. It takes a lot of work with Tinkerbell and the Lost Kids before Peter finally lets go of his adult identity and risks becoming Peter Pan again.

Frankie in *Million Dollar Baby* remains the curmudgeon who refuses to risk putting Maggie into the championship ring. It is only after she and Scrap work on him throughout the second act that he finally lets her take on the tougher, more dangerous opponents.

This is an important point, so don't forget it: The reason your hero will try to maintain his character flaw is that he does not view it as a flaw, but as a defense mechanism.

Let's say that a hero was abused by a family member as a child. Too young to *physically* escape, the young hero escapes *emotionally* by becoming withdrawn.

Later, as an adult, the hero might still be withdrawn because this is how he has learned to deal with life and its vicissitudes. Even though we, as viewers, can see how this withdrawal is hurting the hero, the hero views it as a defense mechanism and will not let go of it.

The hero's flaw is the way in which he deals with life. It's the way he survives life.

EXAMPLES FROM FAMOUS FILMS

In *Million Dollar Baby*, the screenwriter Paul Haggis whips through the list of things to do in the first act:

- The hero, Frankie, and the ally, Scrap, are introduced immediately. Frankie steps in to take care of the boxer Big Willie's cut during a match. Scrap is introduced via his voice-over, as the narrator of the story. We see Frankie's anger and inability to deal with others when he cusses out another man, demeaning him.

- We are introduced to the enabling circumstances immediately—the boxing world where Frankie's fear of intimacy is allowed, and perhaps even encouraged.

- The opponent, Maggie, is introduced in the very next scene as she asks Frankie to manage her. We again see Frankie's flaw as he gruffly and rather rudely tells her he doesn't manage "girls." Now we've seen the flaw expressed twice, so we subconsciously understand that it is deep-seated. Frankie also articulates the theme of the movie when he says, "Girlie, tough ain't enough." We see this later because Frankie is tough, but it has never been enough.

- After the fight, Frankie tells his fighter, Big Willie, that he turned down a title fight for him. It's obvious that he's worried about his fighter getting hurt, and we see the mitigating good quality that makes this hardened old man worth finding out about.

At first it seems that the life-changing event is Big Willie leaving Frankie because he can't stand waiting for a title shot. But that would hardly have changed Frankie's anger and fear of intimacy. In fact, being betrayed would foster even more avoidance of intimacy and trust. No, the real life-changing event is instigated by the opponent, Maggie, who eventually forces Frankie to train her; it comes about thirty-five pages into the story. Frankie has put himself in a position to choose between his fear of intimacy and the opportunity to share his life with this remarkable young woman whose pain matches his own.

OUR STORY

Let's flesh out the life-changing event for Ross, the cowardly Green Beret/accountant in our story. Ross' enabling circumstance is the accounting office of a medium-sized company, so we made the life-changing event take place at the company itself. That way, Ross' enabling circumstance will be directly threatened, which is part of what will motivate him to respond to the life-changing event.

In Chapter 6, we decided that the opponent, Matt, steals millions of dollars in pension money and other funds, without which the company will go broke.

The company employees stand to lose their jobs and their life savings, which are tied up in the company's pension and 401(k) funds.

This is a strong and believable life-changing event. It threatens Ross' enabling circumstances (his job). It forces him to choose between his cowardice (his flaw) and the challenge presented by the life-changing event.

Now the life-changing event kicks the story into the second act with some considerable momentum, drama, jeopardy, and conflict.

Up to this point, we've used the first act to show Ross, his circumstances, his flaw, and his mitigating good qualities. We've introduced the opponent, and showed how Ross has wrapped himself in a set of enabling circumstances in which he can safely operate with his flaw intact. We also showed the other side of the cowardly Ross—the way he beat up the would-be robbers when he went to the bank to make a night deposit.

Now all of it—Ross' entire enabling circumstances, his flaw, his entire life, really—is in jeopardy.

11.

ACT TWO PART ONE

N ote that I've divided Act Two into two parts. That is because Act Two is roughly 60 pages long—twice as long as either Act One or Act Three. Since there is a great prejudice in the industry against a four-act script, I've divided the second act into Act Two, Part One (Chapter 11) and Act Two, Part Two (Chapter 12) so that the script is broken down a little more easily.

DELINEATE THE STORYLINES: OBJECTIVE VS. SUBJECTIVE STORYLINES

The first thing we need to do in the second act is to delineate the storylines. In a well-written story, there are two storylines: the "objective" and the "subjective." Creating two viable, intertwining, mutually supporting storylines is one of the most important elements of storytelling. The objective storyline is the story of the hero's physical struggle to respond to the life-changing event. The subjective storyline is the hero's struggle to overcome his character flaw.

NOTE: The *solution* to the hero's flaw should exist on the subjective level, and definitely not on the *objective* level.

A hero's flaw should always be subjective, or, in other words, personal. If a hero's flaw can be fixed merely by re-arranging some things in the outside world, or on the purely physical level, it's the wrong flaw.

Look at it this way: Every boxing movie is going to be about a boxer trying to be a better boxer, trying to win on the physical level. What differentiates one boxing movie from another, one war movie from another, or one love story from another, is the hero's personal flaw and the journey the hero has to undertake to overcome that flaw on the subjective level.

The subjective level is the level on which the hero works out his problems.

The objective level is the level on which the hero *demonstrates* that he has overcome his flaw. He demonstrates what he has learned on the subjective level.

NOTE: While the resolution of the hero's flaw lies on the subjective level, the commercially viable hook of the movie usually lies on the objective level. The hook is the concept of the movie that is used to sell the movie to studios and to audiences. For example:

> "A little boy finds a space alien in his closet."
>
> "A down-and-out club fighter gets a one-in-a-million shot at the heavyweight championship of the world."
>
> "A suicidal cop is paired with a cop who is mere days from retirement."

All of these are on the objective level. (For more on hooks, see page 156.)

The subjective storyline is usually, to some degree, the search for love. However, it is only when the hero's struggle for love emerges on the *objective* level that the story really starts. This, then, is the inextricable relationship between the objective and subjective storylines in most well-written movies.

There are exceptions. In "cartoon" movies like superhero movies or action films like *Raiders of the Lost Ark*, you can get away with the objective storyline alone, if you make that storyline strong enough. However, please note that even in a superhero film like *Batman Begins*, the writers chose to create a strong subjective storyline to revive the *Batman* franchise.

Another important point: Your hero must have the *ability* to respond to the life-changing event. If your hero is a coward, don't have his life-changing event be that he has to single-handedly defeat the Red Chinese Army.

Yes, to single-handedly defeat the entire Red Chinese Army would certainly be a sign that the hero has overcome his cowardice. However, it is an invalid life-changing event, because it's impossible for any hero to successfully meet the challenge presented.

PICK A STORYLINE, ANY STORYLINE

STOP! Pick six storylines.

Right now, do this exercise—pick six movies and write down the objective and subjective storylines, just to ensure that you really understand the difference between the two different types of storylines.

The Ticking Clock

The objective storyline also often provides the "ticking clock." Although many people sneer at the ticking clock plot device—a deadline that the hero has to meet—it is a powerful tool if used appropriately. After all, stories take place in space and time, so why not make sure the place and time are used to their best advantage?

You may not find the ticking clock in every script, but it is a valuable tool when it's appropriate to the story.

Hero's Emotional Reaction to the Life-Changing Event

The first event in the second act is the hero's *emotional* reaction to the life-changing event. This could be denial, anger, fear, despair, amusement, arrogance, fatalism, whatever.

Hero's Physical Reaction to the Life-Changing Event

The opponent has already taken his first step. He did this by instigating the life-changing event. This event immediately put the hero and opponent into opposition.

Therefore, after an emotional reaction, the hero must *physically* react to the opponent's instigation of the life-changing event. His response is usually to seek out an ally, or he turns to an ally who is already present in his life, in the hope of finding a way to either avoid the life-changing event or to meet it *without having to give up his character flaw*. The irony is that the hero is unconsciously seeking the one person best suited to help him overcome that flaw.

Ally Offers Help

The first thing an ally does is to try to help—after all, that is his main role in the story. He might suggest or agree to a course of action. Remember, however, that the ally is dealing with a hero whose goal is to maintain his flaw while trying to take advantage of the opportunity in the life-changing event. In that sense, then, the hero and ally are in opposition for most of the second act.

Hero Determines the Course of Action

The hero will either accept or reject the course of action. He will accept the course of action as long as it does not threaten his character flaw and his enabling circumstances.

The hero will balk as soon as he does recognize a threat to his character flaw and/or enabling circumstances. If he balks immediately, then the hero's ally might carry out the course of action by himself, and in doing so, shame the hero into joining him, although perhaps too late.

If the hero accepts the course of action because he does not recognize it as a threat, he will balk sometime during the course of action, as soon as the threat to his flaw becomes apparent.

Hero and Ally Instigate
the First Action Against the Opponent

Whatever the hero's initial response to the ally's suggested course of action, whether immediate balking or immediate acceptance, the next step is that the hero and ally instigate the first action against the opponent.

This "attack" on the opponent can take many shapes. In *Rocky*, Mickey and Rocky start training harder and smarter.

In *Wedding Crashers*, which is comedy with romantic themes, Claire is the opponent on the subjective level (Sack is the objective opponent). What she opposes is John wanting only to get laid and still avoid intimacy at any cost. So what does John do? He immediately sets out to seduce her. He compares battle plans with his ally, Jeremy, and they start the attack.

In *Batman Begins*, Ducard is the opponent. How does Bruce begin battling him? By beating his record for hanging onto the side of a wall. Before knowing that he would one day have to battle Ducard, Bruce prepares himself for that battle by striving to outdo Ducard physically.

In *Million Dollar Baby*, Frankie tries to take his speed bag away from Maggie, and in the process tells her she's too old to be a fighter. Now there is an attack!

Opponent Counterattacks and States His Point of View

The opponent reacts to the ally and hero's initial attack by launching a counterattack. In the process, the opponent intentionally or incidentally states his point of view.

Depending on when the hero balks, the balk will cause the hero's ally to react. The ally might react angrily, or certainly with some degree of surprise and confusion. Remember, the ally does not know about the hero's character flaw. The ally does not understand why the hero is balking.

It is up to you to choose when the hero's balk occurs. It often occurs during the hero and ally's first action against the opponent, or during the opponent's first counterattack. This is where the greatest jeopardy and, therefore, the greatest tension and drama exist. This is a dramatic and exciting way to show the hero hindered by his character flaw. It's also a great way to trigger a response by the opponent, which is the next step.

It gives the hero's ally a logical reason to tear into the hero. It also pushes the hero very strongly in the direction of choosing between his flaw and some opportunity—such as the opportunity to regain his self-respect, especially in front of the woman he's attracted to or the boss he wants to impress.

All of this will, at the very least, pressure the hero into admitting he has a flaw and that it might be hindering him.

Ally Confronts Hero About Balk

At this point the hero's ally will confront the hero about his balking, and will either present an ultimatum or simply refuse to work with him anymore. The hero's ally will certainly not want to go through such a balk again (especially if it involved danger)

Hero Renews His Determination to Meet the Life-Changing Event

At this point, the hero may try to give up the opportunity that's presented by the life-changing event. Alternatively, he may be willing to confront the opponent and to reconcile with the hero's ally. This means that the hero will have to renew his determination to meet the challenge of the life-changing event and to take advantage of its inherent opportunity.

Hero Expands His Area of Concern

This is the first instance of the hero expanding his area of concern. There may be other instances—the expansion can take place in several steps. In *Million Dollar Baby*, Frankie begins by caring only about himself and the loss of his daughter. He grows as a person when he expands his area of concern to include Maggie.

In *Batman Begins*, Bruce initially cares only about the guilt that he feels over his parents' death. That's the extent of his area of concern. In Act 2, Part 1, he ends up including the entire city of Gotham in his area of concern.

Hero Confronts His Character Flaw

This is an important point in the story; it is the first time that the hero confronts his character flaw. It's the first time he consciously, willingly decides to try to overcome it, despite the dangers involved, even if they're only emotional dangers.

As I mentioned, you need to apply ingenuity and imagination to your storytelling, which means it's up to you to decide when and how to introduce a story element.

Hero Convinces Ally to Give Him Another Chance

The script will be far too short and unexciting, however, if the hero completely overcomes his character flaw at this point. Instead, he needs to first convince his ally to give him another chance. Second, he needs to take the next physical step against the opponent to prove himself to his ally, as he begins to tackle his character flaw.

This is the moment where the hero pays the price for his balk.

Hero Proves Himself to Ally

The next step is for the hero to prove his renewed determination and trustworthiness to the ally. He does this by taking responsibility for the next step against the opponent. This is the first concrete step in shedding his character flaw.

It is also the first of several steps that occur on the way to the final confrontation between the hero and the opponent in the third act.

Thus, the danger that the hero forces himself to face at this point in the story should have relevance to the danger he faced at the original point of origin, a danger he failed to master at that time. The readers/viewers, as well as our hero, should be reminded of that earlier danger in a very poignant, powerful way. It should make us wonder with dread whether the hero can do better than he did the first time he faced danger of this kind.

Hero Partially Redeems Himself, Bonds With Ally

This act of beginning to handle his character flaw gains the hero some redemption, some "brownie points" with the ally. The ally, mollified, bonds with the hero, realizing that the hero has a character flaw but that he is willing to try to overcome it.

Second Act Confrontation Between Hero and Ally

At the end of the first part of the second act, the hero and ally have a confrontation that will determine the nature of their relationship for the rest of the screenplay. Remember, the hero does not regard his flaw as a flaw, but rather as a necessary way of dealing with the world. Even in the face of a strong life-changing event, the hero will battle to maintain his flaw. He will even resist the ally's attempts to help him overcome that flaw.

It reminds me of a parable told by my good friend, Aaron. A scorpion approaches a river and sees a turtle about to cross. He approaches the turtle who is immediately on guard against the poisonous insect. "Will you carry me across the river on your shell?" the scorpion asks. "Of course not," the turtle replies. "You'll sting me." "No I won't," the scorpion says. "If I sting you, you'll die and I'll drown." The turtle sees the logic in that and lets the scorpion climb atop his shell. Halfway across the river, the scorpion stings the turtle. "Why did you do that?" the turtle cries, feeling the paralysis setting in. "Now we'll both die!" The scorpion shrugs. "I know, but it's just my nature."

Our hero is like that: It's just his nature to resist the help offered to him, because his experience has led him to mistrust such help.

This often leads to an antagonistic relationship between the hero and ally. The ally's job is to help the hero overcome his character flaw. The hero's job is to hold onto his flaw while trying to take advantage of the opportunity offered by the life-changing event.

This conflict between the hero and ally escalates until the middle of the second act (around page sixty, or sixty minutes into the movie) at which time there is a confrontation and dislocation in their relationship. This confrontation can take many forms:

- The ally threatens to withdraw his support unless the hero lets go of his character flaw.

- The ally, with the same flaw as the hero, acts out that flaw so dramatically that it shakes the hero into realizing the danger of his own flaw.

- The ally performs a particularly powerful act as a positive role model, which forces the hero to see the positive outcome he can have if he emulates the ally's behavior.

Whatever form the confrontation takes, it leads to the following actions.

Hero Reveals Part of His Character Flaw to Ally

Through the confrontation, the hero's flaw is revealed to the ally. The ally realizes that the hero's flaw is extremely difficult for the hero to overcome. He offers help, or at least lends a sympathetic ear. The hero accepts the offer, partially, maybe tentatively. He reveals part of his flaw and the reason behind it, but then draws back. It's still too early for him to completely overcome his flaw or even to wholly face it.

Usually this confrontation between hero and ally is positive, bringing them closer and eliminating the struggle between them, allowing them to join against the opponent. Not so in a tragedy, of course, such as *Brokeback Mountain* or *Leaving Las Vegas*. That is because in a tragedy the ally is not successful in breaking through to the hero. For example, Ben in *Leaving Las Vegas* commits suicide as he originally intended, despite Sera giving him her love and showing him that he has something to live for. In *Brokeback Mountain*, Jack tries to get Ennis to "come out" and live his gay life out in the open, but Ennis's fear of being killed is too great.

Ally Makes Demand of Hero

The still-tentative ally will make demands of the hero. The ally may demand that the hero open up to the ally, which is the subjective demand. The ally may demand that the hero let the ally lead the way (since she still doesn't trust him to do so).

When the ally takes control, the ally can become a positive role model for the hero. The hero sees how even someone weaker than he is can still take control even in the face of his own fears.

Ally Reveals Own Struggles

This acting as a role model can be made more powerful if the hero's ally reveals something about himself that makes being a role model more admirable. For example, he may reveal that he has had his own traumas, which makes taking command as difficult for him as it might be for the hero. This allows the hero to realize that he is not alone in his fears and difficulties; it puts things into perspective for our hero.

EXAMPLES FROM FAMOUS FILMS

The objective storyline is the story of the hero's physical struggle to respond to the life-changing event. In *Wedding Crashers*, it's John's attempt to win Claire's heart. In *Million Dollar Baby*, it's Frankie's mission to coach Maggie to the championship. In *As Good as It Gets*, it's Melvin's attempt to win Carol's heart. In *Good Will Hunting*, it's Will's attempt to satisfy Sean and Lambeau so that he can avoid jail time. In *Rocky*, the objective storyline is Rocky Balboa's physical preparation for the boxing match.

The subjective storyline is the hero's struggle to overcome his character flaw. In *Wedding Crashers*, it's John's struggle to overcome his fear of intimacy. In *Million Dollar Baby*, it's Frankie's struggle to overcome his fear of intimacy which is based on his failed relationship with his daughter and his fear of being hurt again.In *Munich*, it's Avner's struggle to reconcile the nature of his task—cold-blooded assassination—with the heroic ideals instilled in him by his heroic father and the admiration he feels for the woman who has asked him to become a murderer: Prime Minister Golda Meir.

In *As Good as It Gets*, the subjective storyline is Melvin's struggle to overcome his mental illness. In *Good Will Hunting*, it's Will's struggle to overcome the anger and fear that became part of him because of his foster father's brutal beatings. In *Rocky*, the subjective storyline is Rocky's struggle to overcome his self-image as a loser.

NOTE: The *solution* to the hero's flaw should exist on the subjective level, and definitely not on the *objective* level.

For example, John lied and manipulated his way into Claire's family in *Wedding Crashers*, and it all blew up in his face. The solution to winning her heart doesn't lie on the level of action or speech or playing more con games on her and her family. It lies in John changing himself on a personal, subjective level, which frees him from his fear of intimacy enough to show his true love and passion for Claire; that is what wins her heart in the end.

Mickey Goldmill trains Rocky on the objective level—how to move, how to punch, how to block, how to build up his endurance. So why isn't that enough? Because Rocky's flaw isn't that he's a lousy boxer. His flaw is personal, which means that it's subjective.

It's on the *subjective* level that John, Frankie, Avner, Melvin, Will, and Rocky have to overcome their flaws.

However, the subjective level is not enough to create a good movie. The chance for a title shot (*Rocky*), the chance to confront the secrets and lies of a family in denial (*Secrets and Lies*), a daughter's death (*Steel Magnolias*)—all of these exist in the objective, external world. Without an objective storyline, you might just as well have a hero sitting alone on a rock, peering out to sea, experiencing great inner conflict, with all of the attendant lack of excitement and involvement for the viewing audience.

In *The Thorn Birds*, the priest's flaw is that he is having a conflict of faith. However, it is only when that conflict expresses itself in the real world in the form of an affair that the story really takes off. A priest having a crisis of faith isn't the hook of the story. A priest having an affair is the hook.

Frankie is obviously searching for love in *Million Dollar Baby*, sending out letter after letter to his estranged daughter, going to church every week searching for God's love. And when he gives in to Maggie's wishes and "pulls the plug" on her breathing tube, it is a selfless act of love.

Avner in *Munich* seeks the love of his hero father, of his Holocaust survivor mother, of his country, and of his country's leader when he agrees to kill people in cold blood.

Will is begging for love in *Good Will Hunting*. As Sean points out to him, Will could have had any job he wanted, and yet he chose one at MIT where it was almost inevitable he would have the chance to show his mathematical acumen and be loved for it. He wants Skylar to love him, so he lies about having twelve brothers so that she won't suspect the truth about the abuse he suffered as a child. After all, as he tells Skylar, he wants her love, not her pity. And he wants that love badly, from Sean, from Skylar, from whoever he can get it from.

Rocky wants to be called a winner instead of a loser, which is a blatant call for love.

It is only when the hero's struggle for love emerges on the *objective* level that the story really starts.

Frankie's desire for his daughter's love isn't enough to make a movie, much less an Oscar-winning one like *Million Dollar Baby*. Frankie taking Maggie under his wing and taking her to the championship makes a movie.

Rocky's desire to be loved, to prove he's not the loser his father told him he was, is not enough to make a movie. Rocky fighting for the championship of the world as a way of proving that he deserves happiness and respect and love—that is an Oscar-winning story.

This is the inextricable relationship between the objective and subjective storylines in most well-written movies.

OUR STORY

The objective storyline for our hero, Ross, is his need to defeat the opponent, Matt, and get Leslie's and the company's money back.

The subjective storyline is Ross' need to overcome his fear and guilt.

The solution to Ross' problem lies on the subjective level simply because he needs to resolve his personal issues before he can have the courage to do anything on the objective level. This is definitely Ross' search for love—he wants to be forgiven for the death of his men. In other words, Ross wants to be loved despite his youthful mistake and the terrible consequences of that mistake.

The first event in the second act is Ross' *emotional* reaction to the life-changing event.

We already know that the life-changing event is Matt ripping the business off for millions, threatening not only

Ross' job and his enabling circumstances, but also the welfare of everyone working for the company, including Leslie, the owner, to whom Ross is strongly attracted.

Now, who is the ally Ross turns to, and what is the first action they take against Matt?

Let's say that Ross and Leslie (the cowardly ex-Green Beret and the beautiful company president) formulate a plan to use the company computers and Ross' computer skills (modern accountants have to be computer savvy) to track down Matt's activities. In the process, they inadvertently alert the computer-savvy Matt, who sends his thugs after Ross and Leslie. This is the opponent's counterattack.

At the moment of the resulting confrontation, Ross freezes—the balk. It is only because of Leslie's quick thinking and courage that they escape Matt's thugs. This is a dramatic and exciting way to show Ross hindered by his character flaw. It's also a great way to trigger a response by Matt, which is the next step. Leslie now has a logical reason to tear into Ross. It also pushes Ross strongly in the direction of choosing between his flaw and some other opportunity—such as the opportunity to regain his self-respect, especially in front of the woman he loves. All of this will, at the very least, pressure Ross into admitting he has a flaw that might be hindering him.

In our story, Leslie's reaction will depend on how she feels about Ross. Does she consider him just another employee? Is she platonically fond of him, maybe even vaguely attracted to him?

One way to handle this situation is to have Ross show his good qualities for the company president to see. This would accomplish two things: Help make Ross likeable, and create a relationship between Leslie and Ross, even if it's casual and non-romantic. We can also use this opportunity to show once more the consequences of Ross' flaw. The company president can really like Ross and even find him physically attractive, but she can equally be put off by Ross' character flaw—his meekness and fear.

Now the company president has her suspicions confirmed when Ross balks in the face of the opponent, Matt. Leslie, disappointed and already upset over the loss of the company's money, confronts Ross for risking their lives with his balk. She refuses to trust him anymore. She leaves him behind as she goes on by herself, trying to track down and confront Matt. Ross learns that Leslie has gone on without him, which places her in danger, and he is shamed into going after her with renewed determination. Now it's not just his own welfare that he's trying to protect, but the welfare of someone he cares about.

This is the first instance of Ross expanding his area of concern. There may be other instances—the expansion can take place in several steps. For example, we can have Ross and Leslie discover that the opponent, Matt, plans to use the stolen money to buy a bomb to kill a bunch of people. This may be too melodramatic, but it certainly does raise the jeopardy dramatically and forces Ross to expand his area of concern.

Or, it can be simpler—Ross expands his area of concern to include Leslie and later expands it to include the other employees, who stand to lose everything they own because of the theft of their pension funds, IRAs, 401(k)s, whatever.

Or, the expansion of the area of concern can be Ross realizing that, as Rick says in *Casablanca*, "I'm no good at being noble, but it don't take much to see that the problems of three little people don't amount to a hill of beans in this crazy world." Or as Gracie says in *Miss Congeniality*: "Hello! Get over yourself!"

Ross catches up to Leslie and tries to get her to give him a second chance, in the same way that Frankie in *Million Dollar Baby* practically climbs into the ring in the middle of the fight to get a second chance to manage Maggie. It's up to us to decide if Leslie takes Ross back as easily as Maggie takes Frankie back, but my feeling is that she's going to be tentative about it, mistrustful of this cowardly hero of hers.

The point of origin of Ross' character flaw had to do with Ross being trapped in an enclosed space by an enemy. There was no way out. He lost one ally after another. Finally he snapped, costing the lives of at least one of his remaining allies. Panicking, Ross ordered an untimely retreat under fire. We need to remember this point of origin. Why? Because it informs the rest of the story. It's the cause of his flaw. Reconciling that original situation is the only way Ross can overcome his flaw.

This is also the point at which the still-tentative Leslie will make demands of Ross. She may demand that he open up to her, which is the subjective demand. She may demand that he let her lead the way (since she still doesn't trust him to do so). Leslie's control of the situation can make her a positive role model for Ross. He sees how the physically weaker Leslie takes control even in the face of her own fears.

Now begins a series of actions by Ross and Leslie, who are united and no longer at odds. These actions bring Ross closer to a confrontation with Matt, which will resemble the original challenge. This will become Ross' chance to make a new, *re*defining decision. As the physical, objective steps are taken, steps have to be taken on the subjective, personal level as well, to prepare Ross to make a different decision than the one he made in the past.

12.

ACT TWO
PaRT TWO

Now we begin the second part of Act Two. This part of the act allows the hero to make a choice and deal with the consequences. The hero's flaw and the hero's ally play heavily in the plot here.

The Hero's Choice

After the second act confrontation, the hero has a choice. He can hold onto the character flaw and give up any chance of successfully responding to the life-changing event. Or he can finally open up to his ally.

Think of the character flaw as a suit of armor. Yes, it protects the hero from having to face his past, and the pain therein. However, it also keeps out the good stuff and locks the hero inside. Now think of the life-changing event as a swimming pool into which the scriptwriter (actually the opponent) pushes the armor-clad hero. The danger of drowning is increased by the very suit of armor that earlier had seemed like protection.

This is the function of the life-changing event—to magnify the negative consequences of the character flaw. That suit of armor was always heavy for the hero to carry around, but now its heaviness can kill him.

Initially, the hero responds to the life-changing event by trying to find a way to rescue himself while still wearing the suit of armor. When it becomes clear that there is no such way, he reluctantly begins to shed the suit of armor. However, still afraid of what is waiting for him on the other side of that protective armor, he takes off the smallest parts of the armor first. He hangs onto as much protection as he can, for as long as he can.

Maybe the hero takes off an armored boot first, because at least that way his heart is still protected.

Maybe he'll take off a chain mail glove, and maybe even, eventually, his helmet, but still he retains his torso armor so that his heart, at least, will remain protected.

Then, at some point, the hero has to make the final commitment to stave off drowning. He casts off the last piece of armor (a.k.a. the character flaw). In so doing, he is able to float to the surface, free of the dead weight. He is free, also, to do battle with the opponent who pushed him into the water to begin with. (Remember, it's usually the opponent who instigates the life-changing event.)

From the moment of that second act confrontation between ally and hero, from the moment he begins to take off that armor, there is an acceleration toward the final battle with the opponent. The hero and ally are now working together. The hero is much closer to overcoming his flaw. And, although the opponent is still increasing the stakes and jeopardy, the hero is also getting stronger.

Although by the end of the second act we still can't be sure that the hero will win, we know that he has at least a *chance* of winning because he is no longer encumbered by his flaw, thanks to the work of the ally.

Hero and Ally Unite Against the Opponent

Now begins a series of actions by the hero and hero's ally, who are now united. These actions bring the hero closer to a confrontation with the opponent, a confrontation that resembles the original challenge. This will become the hero's chance to make a new, redefining, decision.

As physical, objective steps are taken, steps also have to be taken on the subjective, personal level to prepare the hero to make a different decision than the one he made in the past. One solution is for our hero to become increasingly intimate (not necessarily romantically intimate) with the ally, growing to care enough about her to want to include her in his area of concern. The combination, then, is: a growing affection and/or respect for the hero's ally; a desire to earn the hero's ally's respect; and a realization that the hero's ally has already done something similar to what the hero is afraid to do.

The goal is to make gaining the ally's respect more important to the hero than maintaining his character flaw. Alternatively, you can view it as making it just too humiliating for the hero to maintain his flaw in the face of the ally's strength.

Hero Expands His Area of Concern Wider

By now it's become clear that the hero has expanded his area of concern even wider, quite a common occurrence in a film. This is because the ally, in trying to convince the hero to help, has made him or her realize what is at stake and who is at risk.

Remember, as we explained earlier, the area of concern is whatever and whomever the hero cares most about. For example, in *Wedding Crashers*, John and Jeremy both begin by caring only about their own pleasure—seducing women at weddings because they are more vulnerable to John and Jeremy's lies and seductions. By the end of the film, both men have grown to care about others—at the very least about the women they initially set out to cold-heartedly seduce: Claire and Gloria.

Opponent Counters Hero and Ally, the Unraveling

During the second act, the opponent counters each of the hero and ally's actions. The stakes, jeopardy, and tension rise steadily on an objective level. This can take any number of forms, of course.

Now comes what I call the unraveling. The unraveling should occur when the hero has the most to lose. In fact, the hero should have as much to lose now as he had at the point of origin, simply because in some ways he's brought himself back to that point of origin.

If things go wrong now, the repercussions are greater than they would be at any other time in his life since the original point of origin. He has the opportunity to react in either the same manner as he did at the point of origin (and thus perpetuate his flaw), or in a different manner that might allow him to redeem himself and resolve his flaw.

Opponent Increases Area of Threat

The opponent increases his area of threat just as the hero has expanded his area of concern. The two are related. The opponent's area of threat is, in essence, his *reach*—the extent to which he can influence (and perhaps threaten) others.

For example, in *Million Dollar Baby*, the opponent is Maggie, even though she's the nicest person in the film, with the possible exception of Scrap. She opposes Frankie in remaining the withdrawn, crusty curmudgeon he's become. Initially she is able only to annoy him, as she pounds away ineffectively at the speed bag, day after day. But slowly her influence (her area of threat) grows, and we see that she is getting to Frankie, making him break down and expose himself until finally she forces him to train her—and to love her.

Now, why is that a threat? Because it IS a threat—to Frankie's flaw, to the defenses he erected in order to avoid being hurt again.

Suddenly the hero is right back at the point of origin. Meanwhile, the threat increases and everything depends on his making the right decision.

Hero Breaks His Own Rules

The hero often responds to this pressure by acting counter to his own rules of conduct and morality in a desperate bid to defeat the opponent. It is at this moment that the hero and opponent are most alike, with one exception: The hero is breaking his own rules, but the opponent is actually *following* his own rules—same actions, different rules.

The important thing here is that the "immoral" act the hero performs does not work. That failure leaves the hero apparently defeated; if even breaking his own rules of conduct fails against the opponent, then the hero is lost—or so it seems.

Opponent Performs Act Forcing Hero to Completely Abandon His Flaw

The danger is escalated now by having the opponent perform an act that cannot be responded to without the hero completely abandoning his flaw. For instance, what if the opponent puts the hero's ally in peril as well? This might, admittedly, be overkill, but it's exciting overkill.

Hero Learns True Danger

This is the point that we have been working toward during the entire script—the point at which the hero either has to completely abandon his flaw or else perish—physically or emotionally. This is the low point for the hero in this story, his moment of greatest peril and also, paradoxically, his moment of greatest opportunity.

Second Circumstance, Challenge, Decision, Self-Definition, and Emotional State

Now, in rapid order, the hero undergoes a second circumstance, a second challenge, a second decision, a second self-definition, and a second emotional state. He will completely overcome his character flaw. He will adopt a new behavior to replace the old behavior.

Here, many heroes have to revisit the past and relive that moment that was so traumatic that he adopted a flaw to protect against it. The challenge comes, though, when the hero has to find a way out of a seemingly hopeless situation. In the original situation years before, his decision led to bad things. The hero needs a way out, but it has to be a path that seems as dangerous as the original situation seemed so many years before.

The last time the hero made that kind of choice, he was wrong. Can he overcome the paralysis that will surely grip him? Can he make that same kind of decision, and will it be the right one this time?

His decision, if correct, will result in a second self-definition. This self-definition will be that the hero is courageous rather than cowardly, or generous rather than greedy—whatever the character arc needs to be, given your story.

No greater courage could be required than to make this decision, knowing that the last such decision damaged his life for years.

Final Expansion of Hero's Area of Concern

The hero finally overcomes his character flaw, his enabling circumstances, and everything that originally led up to that expression and circumstance. It's also the hero's final expansion of his area of concern. He may have been willing to allow himself to perish, but he isn't willing to let someone else die.

The Point of No Return

There is occasionally one more important event before the end of the second part of the second act: the point of no return. This is the point at which the hero is tempted to backslide. If the hero can overcome this final bout of self-doubt, he will be beyond the point of no return and will head straight into battle with the opponent.

Note that the point of no return is sometimes less of a temptation to backslide than a confirmation of the hero overcoming his flaw. The opportunity to backslide is presented, and the hero confirms his growth by refusing the opportunity.

EXAMPLES FROM FAMOUS FILMS

Melvin doesn't win Carol's heart in *As Good as It Gets* by taking her on another car trip or paying for her son's medical needs. He does it by changing on a personal level, by starting to overcome his psychological demons with the help of Simon. And he knows he's ready to battle Carol for her heart when he goes to the door and realizes that he's forgotten to lock the countless locks on the door.

Melvin merely wanting Carol's love isn't enough to make a movie. Watching him let his guard down to care for Simon's dog and then seeing his journey to becoming a humane, caring person: that makes a hell of a movie. Another Oscar winner, in fact.

OUR STORY

Ross is both an accountant and a risk-taker. So let's show it even more. After he knocks out the hoodlums who try to steal the company payroll from him, he goes to an extreme sports park. There he rock-climbs, hang-glides, and does obstacle courses, all of which show us his extreme physical abilities.

However, we can't forget Ross' flaw. So, at the end of Ross' display of physical prowess, he is confronted by someone at the park—a bully who wants to push in front of Ross at the snack shop or out on one of the courses. Ross backs down, and once again we're reminded of his character flaw. We now have an interesting context in which to place that fear: the context of Ross' amazing physical abilities.

Let's build this up even more. What if, during the original incident at the point of origin (the war), Ross was not just a soldier, but also the *leader* of the squad of Green Berets trapped by the enemy? He ordered his men to break out and retreat, and in the process they were all slaughtered except for Ross. Even though it was a well-meant order, Ross sees it as an act of cowardice that cost his men their lives. If he hadn't been so afraid, hadn't ordered the cowardly retreat...

Let's make this even worse for Ross: Within an hour of his men getting killed, reinforcements arrived. If Ross had waited, his men would still be alive. If that doesn't create a flaw in your character, nothing will!

Ross has a combination of computer savvy, physical prowess, military know-how, *and* command experience, so he is at least theoretically able to help himself and the other employees, However, he may only be willing to take that risk for Leslie's sake. His area of concern is larger, but not as large as it could be.

Let's say that Ross, trying to redeem himself in front of Leslie, does agree to lead the other employees against Matt to recover the stolen money and save the company. He organizes a combination "sting" and "commando" operation. He uses the computer eggheads in the company's accounting division to set up a computer sting operation. Meanwhile, he simultaneously organizes his friends from the extreme sports park into a paramilitary unit to invade Matt's headquarters. Matt is also a computer whiz, and Ross and Leslie have already tried to track him down using the computer, so Matt will be expecting another computer attack. Ross hopes, however, that Matt won't expect to have to simultaneously fend off a *physical* assault, especially since Matt thinks of Ross as a coward and Leslie as "just a woman."

Ross sets his accounting/computing team to perform a frontal computer assault on Matt's computer system. Then he leads his extreme sports team on a physical raid of Matt's offices: *The Sting* meets *Sneakers* meets *The Dirty Dozen*.

There's going to be ample chance here for Ross to come up against his character flaw. If he led his men to death at the point of origin, imagine the risk he takes in organizing another team of men on a similarly dangerous mission.

In fact, to make the mission even more dangerous, let's make Matt a mobster, a casino owner who has stolen Leslie's money and electronically merged it with his own casino's finances to avoid being killed by his mobster bosses for having lost a huge amount of money from the casino.

The "sting" part of the operation could be to sucker Matt into making a mistake that gets him into trouble with his mob bosses. The risk to Ross, of course, is that the mob is exactly the wrong type of people to mess with, even if you are an ex-Green Beret.

Plus, let's put the casino on Indian land. Such land is usually isolated, increasing the difficulty of physically breaking into the building or even approaching it without being seen.

The point is that Ross tries to combine his own skills with those of his accounting and adrenalin-junkie friends in an extremely risky assault on Matt's stronghold. It is a combination sting operation/commando raid that carries the risk of his screwing up again, with lives on the line—again.

By the way, there's going to have to be some kind of justification for why Ross and Leslie don't just call the cops. It could be a lack of proof, or perhaps collusion between Matt and the cops. It doesn't matter what it is, as long as it believably makes it necessary for Leslie and Ross to take action on their own.

You can even throw in a twist. What if Leslie is actually, secretly, Matt's lover? She had planned to loot her own company with Matt, but was then betrayed at the last moment. This is why she turned to Ross, hoping to play on his "niceness" and computer skills to help recover the money. The Green Beret skills, which she hadn't known about, were just a bonus.

This twist could be something that Ross discovers at the very end when Leslie turns on him. Or, it could be something he has to get over in order to trust and work with Leslie to get the company's money back. Either way would work.

An example of this kind of scenario is *The Verdict* with Paul Newman, in which the woman he falls in love with turns out to be a spy for the opposing attorneys.

By now it's clear that Ross has expanded his area of concern even wider, to include not just Leslie, but all of the men he has organized to attack Matt, as well as the employees of the company. Leslie, in trying to convince Ross to help, has made him realize what is at stake and who is at risk.

The point of origin for Ross occurred during the war, when he led a group of soldiers against the enemy and, ultimately, to their deaths. Now here he is, leading a group of extreme athletes against a dangerous enemy. If things go wrong now, the repercussions are greater than they would be at any other time in his life since the original point of origin. This is an opportunity to react in either the same manner as he did at the point of origin (and thus perpetuate his flaw), or to choose a different manner that will redeem him and resolve his flaw.

We create the unraveling by having Ross start to lose his men. Maybe not literally—maybe they get trapped in the casino and cut off. They know they're going to be found out because there's a ticking clock: Ross' team must be out by a certain time or they will be discovered. Suddenly Ross is back at the point of origin, leading a team of men into a trap, then having to decide what to do to save them. Meanwhile, the threat increases and everything depends on his making the right decision.

Matt has trapped all of Ross' men in the casino. Ross has seemingly blown his last chance to save them. We can escalate the danger even more now by having Matt perform an act that cannot be responded to without Ross completely abandoning his flaw.

What can that act be? Well, what if Matt locks everyone—his own men, the casino patrons, and the hero and his men—in the casino along with a huge bomb that is big enough to destroy the casino and everyone in it?

And, what if Matt also puts Leslie in peril, planting a similar bomb in her company headquarters building? Matt is determined to eliminate anyone who might be able to track him down.

This might, admittedly, be overkill, but it's exciting overkill. If Ross, trapped in the casino and cut off from Leslie, is going to survive and save the men he got involved in this caper, he must become the leader he failed to be at the point of origin. However, he does not yet know about the bombs. That's the *next* escalation.

Ross learns, in succession, that: there is a bomb that will kill him and his extreme-sport weekend warriors; the bomb will also kill Matt's own men and the innocent bystanders patronizing the casino; a second bomb will kill Leslie and all the company employees that he assigned to break into Matt's computer system. Worse, Ross realizes that this is partly his fault for having brought the extreme athletes, company employees, and Leslie into the battle with Matt.

This is the point that we have been working toward during the entire script— the point at which Ross either has to completely abandon his flaw or else perish— physically or emotionally.

We see many heroes revisit the past at this point, remembering a moment that was so traumatic that they adopted the flaw to protect themselves against it. In our story, this second circumstance and second challenge is the attack on the casino that trapped Ross and his team inside. This is equivalent to the original circumstance, in which Ross led his men in an attack during the war. The second decision arises out of the need to save his men once they're trapped in the casino, which parallels Ross' original decision, which was to either fight or flee.

The challenge comes when Ross has to find a way out of a seemingly hopeless situation. In the original situation years before, his decision was to flee under enemy fire. That decision got his men killed and led to years of guilt, self-doubt, and hiding. Now Ross is trapped in the casino. We have to give him a way out, but it has to be an escape that is as dangerous as the original situation seemed so many years before. He has to decide once again: Is it better to wait for help, or to try a risky escape?

The choice is the same: Wait in the casino (foxhole/bunker) hoping that someone will save them, or take a risk so great that it seems suicidal. The last time Ross made that kind of choice, he was wrong. Can he make the same kind of decision, and will it be the right one this time?

This decision, if correct, will result in a second self definition. This self-definition will be that Ross is courageous rather than cowardly, a leader instead of a loser. No greater courage is required of a man than to make this decision, knowing that the last such decision killed the men who depended on him for their lives. Finally, this decision, if correct, will lead to a new emotional state: courage and a feeling of power and leadership.

Ross, determined to redeem himself and save his men, acts decisively, as a leader.

Ross and his men are trapped in the casino vault area. There is one way out, but it is blocked by a number of casino security guards working for Matt. Ross realizes he is in the same situation, and he freezes. Another of the extreme athletes, frustrated by Ross' inaction, takes matters in his own hands and braves the security guard's fire in order to escape. At the last second, Ross comes to the extreme athlete's rescue, barely saving him from being killed.

Ross made a decision, and although they are still trapped within the casino vaults, at least he has thrown his hat into the ring. He doesn't know how he's going to get his men out, but finally he is determined to use his considerable skills and leadership ability to do so. He may have been willing to die rather than make the decision, but he wasn't willing to let someone else die.

The point of no return is where Ross is tempted to backslide. If he can overcome this final bout of self-doubt, he will head straight into battle with Matt.

Now we're ready for the final act.

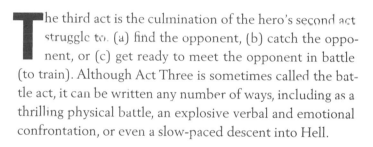

13.

ACT THREE

The third act is the culmination of the hero's second act struggle to: (a) find the opponent, (b) catch the opponent, or (c) get ready to meet the opponent in battle (to train). Although Act Three is sometimes called the battle act, it can be written any number of ways, including as a thrilling physical battle, an explosive verbal and emotional confrontation, or even a slow-paced descent into Hell.

All or Nothing

At the beginning of the third act, it's all or nothing, and it should feel like all or nothing, winner-take-all. The stakes are at their highest; the jeopardy, tension, conflict, and drama should be at their peak. This act should have the feel of a rush to finality or perhaps a slow fall into inevitable tragedy.

Damage to Hero Mounts

In this final act, the damage to the hero mounts, emotionally and/or physically. The result of the struggle between

---

the hero and opponent hangs in the balance. We should not know who wins until the final moments of the film—unless there is a "tag" scene at the end, which can be used to tie up loose ends. Or unless it's a tragedy and failure is inevitable.

The Low Point

This is the low point for the hero. This is the point where it seems like everything that could have gone wrong already has gone wrong, and there is apparently no way to succeed.

In *Million Dollar Baby*, the low point is probably when Frankie learns from the doctors that Maggie is permanently paralyzed. In *Wedding Crashers*, it's when John and Jeremy are exposed as liars by Sack, and John apparently loses any chance he has to be with Claire. In *Batman Begins*, it's when Batman is pinned under a beam in a burning building after having been beaten by his opponent.

Hero Discovers a Way to Fight Back

The hero, through his own actions or with the aid of the ally, finds a way to fight back. In *Million Dollar Baby*, Frankie realizes that he has the strength to take care of Maggie even with her disability. He takes charge, realizing the love he has for this young woman who reminds him so much of his own daughter, and realizing how strong and determined that love makes him. He finally learns how to fight back with love.

In *Wedding Crashers*, John learns of Claire and Sack's wedding and decides he's going to crash one more wedding—theirs!

Audience Discovers Full Extent of Opponent's Threat

Just as the hero finds what he thinks he needs, the audience learns something that the hero cannot know yet. The full extent of the opponent's threat becomes clear. This is something new that increases the danger even more. It's also something the hero needs to know or else he's going to lose and/or perish.

This step turns up the tension tremendously. Imagine, as an audience member, that you've just seen the opponent's second gun, but the hero hasn't. You know that unless the hero learns about the second gun, the opponent will destroy him. This drives you crazy in a thrilling way. This is when viewers yell at the screen, trying to warn the hero. Now *that* is being involved in a movie.

Hero Learns of Increased Threat
Then, just before it will destroy him, the hero discovers what we already know about the opponent's true threat. We breathe again, wiping our foreheads and feeling the exciting tingle of fear dissipating in our bellies. The hero is safe … for now.

The Final Battle
The final battle is the last confrontation between the hero and opponent, the time when the subjective and objective storylines finally tip one way or the other, but not necessarily the same way.

Hero Fully Engages Opponent
Now the hero knows the real and complete danger. It's daunting, but at least he knows what he's dealing with, and he makes his plan accordingly.

Hero Restates Point of View
Somewhere in this section the opponent needs to reaffirm his point of view. The hero needs to reaffirm his, too, in the

face of the opponent's point of view. This could be a fascinating and ironic way to show how similar and yet different the opponent is from the hero.

Hero Defeats or is Defeated by Opponent

Depending on whether it's a tragedy such as *Macbeth* or *Brokeback Mountain*, or a comedy such as *Wedding Crashers*, the hero will, at this point, complete the struggle by either defeating or being defeated by the opponent.

Someone once said that an argument (or confrontation) is nothing but an exchange of values. It's that way between the hero and opponent during the final showdown. As they battle, the opponent should reaffirm his point of view. After all, the clash in their points of view is what this story is all about. If they both had the same point of view, they'd be allies, not opponents.

The opponent denigrates the hero's point of view. He might tell the hero that he is a loser because he lets himself be ruled by guilt and obedience to "the rules." The opponent believes that he has won because he's willing to do whatever is *necessary* to win.

The hero must reply by reaffirming *his* belief.

At this point the opponent can point out the hero's culpability. After all, this came about because of the hero's flaw, and he has to take responsibility for that, right? In fact, the hero must admit to his culpability here, or he really hasn't completely overcome his flaw. However, the hero uses his own culpability as the very *reason* he is sticking to his point of view. After all, he needs to make amends for his culpability. This is the point at which the hero's and opponent's points of view are most clearly and strongly stated.

The philosophical and emotional conflict greatly deepens. That conflict makes the *physical* conflict between the hero and opponent more meaningful.

One character emerges triumphant—at least objectively.

Hero, Changed by the Events in the Story, Faces The Future
The hero now faces the future as a very different person.

Optional Final Twist
There is another step that can be taken to intensify the third act. That twist is up to you, the author, and can take any form imaginable as long as it's consistent with the story and the characters. If Indiana Jones suddenly became a priest at the end of *Raiders of the Lost Ark*, it would certainly be a twist, but one that would not play, given Indy and the circumstances of the story.

This twist should raise the emotional stakes of the final battle and lend a certain edge or perhaps even irony to the whole act.

EXAMPLES FROM FAMOUS FILMS

Examples of this third act are the final series of fight scenes in *Rocky* and the dinner scene in *Secrets and Lies*.

In *Brokeback Mountain*, the third act is the slow unfolding of inevitable tragedy. After Jack says, "I wish I knew how to quit you," Ennis has the chance to fight for what he wants. His memories of his father showing him the fatally beaten gay man are too strong; his fear is too strong, so Ennis drives away from Jack for the last time. When Ennis learns of Jack's death, he has two choices; he can dwell in the tragedy or he can finally overcome his flaw. It is too late for his love with Jack to be anything but tragic, but Ennis learns through loss that he has to open himself up more to people, and ends the movie with the hope of eventually having a relationship with his estranged daughter again.

In *Million Dollar Baby*, the third act is *not* the fight for the world championship. The third act in this film begins at the end of the boxing battle. The *real* battle begins when Maggie falls on the stool and breaks her neck, becoming paralyzed for life. At that moment Frankie's battle starts: the battle to open up completely to Maggie, beginning with supporting her as she lies paralyzed in the hospital and ending with the final decision he makes on her behalf.

Leaving Las Vegas and *Brokeback Mountain* are great examples of films in which the heroes literally end up with nothing—although they had, at one point, been given the opportunity to have lives with people who loved them.

Even in films that are not tragedies, the final act, or the battle, can be slow-paced, as in Oliver Stone's *World Trade Center*, where the final act is the grinding battle to survive until help arrives.

There are obvious examples, like in *Rocky* and even *World Trade Center*, in which the heroes become more and more damaged—beaten up by the world champion, or dangerously dehydrated while lying under the weight of the World Trade Center rubble. There is also emotional damage, such as that suffered by Frankie in *Million Dollar Baby* as he's forced to watch Maggie, the young woman he loves like a daughter, lying in a bed permanently paralyzed, starting to lose limbs. She finally asks him to put her out of her misery.

OUR STORY

So where are we so far? Ross set his accounting/computer whizzes to do an electronic frontal assault on Matt's computer system. As a back-up plan and/or diversion, Ross takes his troop of extreme athletes into the casino to physically recover the equivalent amount of stolen money from the casino vaults. Ross and his troops "stealth" their way into the casino, while the accountant computer geeks attack electronically.

Something goes wrong. Ross and his troops are trapped inside. They discover that instead of a few million dollars in gambling money, the casino has billions of dollars in cash, securities, and electronic deposits linked to banks around the world. It's bigger than they could have imagined.

The accountant geeks are able to manipulate the computer-operated security system to keep the casino guards from knowing that he and his men are inside the vault area of the casino. However, Ross and his men are cut off from communicating with Leslie or anyone else.

Now the truth about the casino is clear: It is the headquarters for a national militia group of unbelievable proportions. Matt isn't part of the mob like we had thought; he's part of something more dangerous. The militia has stolen huge amounts of money and stockpiled it over a period of years. They intend to use the money to destabilize the economy and take over the government surreptitiously by bankrupting both political parties and blackmailing politicians and financial leaders.

This is the final expansion of Ross' area of concern. The story began as his attempt to save or rescue his own enabling circumstances—his pension funds and his job. However, it quickly became a concern for Leslie, then for the other employees, then his troop of extreme athletes, and now, finally, for the entire country.

We can add one more bit of jeopardy to supply additional concreteness and immediacy to the danger. Matt is planning to betray his own people. He's set a huge explosive device meant to destroy the casino and all the militia members, since he arranged for all his followers to be in the casino for a meeting. Matt has suckered everybody. He has billions of dollars he's about to transfer to Swiss banks. He'll then blow up the casino with all the militia personnel, casino employees, and patrons to make it look as if a rival group set off the explosion. Meanwhile, Matt plans to sneak off to Europe with his fortune and a new identity, with no militia members left to track him down.

This is the low point for Ross. Matt seals off the casino, locking the militiamen, casino patrons, Ross, and his team inside with the bomb. Then Matt leaves for the airport.

It seems hopeless. There is no way out for Ross and the others in the fortified, locked-up casino. Then Ross finds or learns something, something that gives him a chance—a small chance, perhaps, but a chance.

However, just as Ross learns or finds what he thinks he needs, the audience (but not Ross) learns something else. The audience learns the full extent of Matt's threat. This is something new that increases the danger even more. It's also something Ross needs to know or else he's going to lose or perish.

This step turns up the tension tremendously.

Say, for instance, that Ross learns that there is a way out—a ventilation crawlway. Or maybe a door is hidden in an unnoticed area of the vault. What he *doesn't* know, though, is that Matt rigged the door to detonate as soon as it is opened. We, the audience, know about the bomb, but Ross doesn't. As he reaches for the door, we hold our breath, wanting to scream at him not to open that damned door!

But let's turn up the jeopardy and tension even more. Let's say that just before Ross finds the crawlway he reaches Leslie on a cell phone for a few moments of static-marred words. Leslie is only able to say that she has alerted the police and the FBI and that they are on their way. Then the phone goes dead.

Ross is right back where he was years before. He is responsible for a band of people that he is leading. There is the threat of death at their doorstep, about to explode at any second. Help is on the way, but the casino is so isolated that there's no telling how long it will take to get there. Does Ross hold on, hoping that the help arrives before the bomb goes off? Does he risk getting his people out of harm's way? Remember, the last time he made a decision, he got a lot of people killed.

Then things get even worse—Ross discovers a possible way out, but it is so dangerous that it's like the danger involved in fleeing to safety by placing one's back to enemy fire. Now Ross has a real choice, and he decides to take the chance.

Then we, the audience, have made our own discovery about the full threat that Matt presents—those explosives are rigged to go off if the door is opened. Ross has found a form of possible, though extremely dangerous, escape. We see the bomb (literal or figurative) on the other side of that escape route, set to go off.

Then, just before it will destroy him, Ross discovers what we already know about Matt's true threat: There is a bomb on the other side of the door. We breathe again, wiping our foreheads and feeling the exciting tingle of fear dissipating in our bellies. Ross is safe ... for now.

Now Ross knows the real and complete danger. It's daunting, but at least he knows what he's dealing with, and he makes his plan accordingly. In our story Ross does not engage Matt directly, but he does fully engage Matt's guards and militiamen and the traps left by Matt.

Ross handles the physical task of getting out of the casino and/or defusing the bomb. Meanwhile, the company president uses her own computer geeks to track the money being transferred to Switzerland, or maybe to retrieve it from Switzerland. She also has them tracking Matt electronically—through credit cards, taxi services, airline reservations. This can become a great scene if Matt foresaw the possibility of being tracked and created a spider web of identities and tickets so that Leslie has to track down every lead, frantically trying to figure out his real itinerary and alert the police at the same time.

We can intercut between Ross trying to get out alive, Matt trying to escape, and Leslie tracking Matt down through a web of ATMs, credit card receipts, etc. Meanwhile, Leslie's computer geeks are tracking the billions Matt has deposited in Swiss banks.

Somewhere in here, though, we need a couple of other elements: Matt needs to reaffirm his point of view. Ross needs to reaffirm his, too, in the face of Matt's point of view.

At some point Matt can call attention to Ross' culpability: Matt would never have been able to do what he had done if Ross hadn't been too afraid to stop him. This is like the Edmund Burke quote: "All that is necessary for the triumph of evil is that good men do nothing." We could set this up by giving Ross a chance early in the script to find out what Matt is really up to, but have him be afraid to become involved. Ross must admit to his culpability here, or else he hasn't completely overcome his flaw. However, Ross uses his own culpability as the very reason he is sticking to his point of view. After all, he needs to make amends for his culpability.

This is the point at which Ross' and Matt's points of view are most clearly and strongly stated. One of those points of view emerges triumphant. We may see Ross' point of view emerge triumph more gradually, as we watch Matt's disintegrating during his attempt to flee.

Since Ross does not directly engage Matt in our particular story, we can do this by proxy: Matt's second-in-command is a woman who passionately believes in the militia movement and its supposed ideals. She directly opposes Ross as he tries to escape. She also represents what Ross once thought he could be when he was a Green Beret: a loyal patriot willing to risk death for her beliefs.

Let's add something even more: while Ross is battling the second-in-command to try to get out of the casino alive without setting off the bomb, Matt is fleeing. He takes a cab to the airport, maybe stopping off at a bank to arrange a last-minute transfer of funds. However, as he flees, Matt begins to be haunted by the full impact of what he is doing—the mass murder he is about to commit not only against his enemies, but also against his own people who have trusted him with their very lives.

This could be a fascinating and ironic way of showing how similar and yet different Matt is from Ross. The opponent has gotten screwed somehow in the past and thought that justified his actions. But the farther he gets from the casino and the closer to freedom, the more he becomes like Ross, a man overwhelmed by guilt for what he has set in motion and the lives that will be destroyed by his actions. And as we see him start to crumble, we contrast him with Ross, who has somehow found the courage and redemption he never thought he could. It would be a nice visual contrast without even saying it, just showing it.

Ross cannot disarm the bomb. However, he does find a way out, and gets everyone else out before the bomb goes off. Meanwhile, Leslie tracks down both the money and Matt, and arrives at the airport in time to watch his arrest.

Then Ross gets to a phone and calls Leslie to warn her of the second bomb (if she doesn't already know about it). She successfully evacuates her own building just before it is destroyed by the blast. At this point, they can live happily ever after.

Unless... we decide to implement that little twist we described earlier. You know the one—Leslie is Matt's former lover who was betrayed by him and used Ross to get revenge—and the money.

We can have Leslie arrested. Alternatively, maybe she doesn't get arrested. Maybe instead, Ross walks away from her in disgust or simply from a brokenhearted realization that as much as he loves her, he'll never be able to trust her.

One character has emerged triumphant—at least objectively. Ross now faces the future as a very different person.

WRITING WITH HEART

The following article originally appeared on Scriptmag's e-zine. Although it is a review of a specific film, the points made in the article can be used to improve your own writing.

I often write about structure, but there is something just as important in making good movies: heart. Not schmaltz, although if you have to choose between schmaltz and meaningless violence, sexploitation, racism, etc., I'll take good old-fashioned schmaltz any time.

Two semi-recent movies serve as good examples of heart emerging triumphant despite structural weaknesses: *The Majestic* and *Joe Somebody*. Unfortunately, the same people who champion the worst Hollywood movies have decided that these two feel-good movies are sub par. Too bad, since we could use more structurally flawed but well-meant movies like these. Better this than *Friday the Thirteenth Part 28*, *Independence Day 14*, or *Home Alone 35*.

The problems with *The Majestic* center on the fact that no one could possibly mistake Jim Carrey for the town's favorite son and war hero. Why? Well, the filmmakers make a huge error at the end of the movie: they have Matt Damon's voice read the war hero's last letter home. Why? Because even they knew how impossibly coincidental it would be for Jim Carrey to not only look exactly like the war hero, but also to have the exact same voice, accent, inflections, timbre, vocabulary, etc.

Worse, the war hero was a star football player. I was no star, but I played high school ball, and I can tell you that I still bear physical scars from it. There is no way that the war hero would not have had scars from his ball playing days, not to mention simply from being a young boy playing rough. I don't know how many scars I have from falling out of trees, running into immovable objects, playing football, karate, weightlifting, whatever. It would have been easy for the war hero's father to have simply looked for one of these scars to confirm Jim Carrey's character's true identity.

That said, the film speaks of heroism, of real family values, where an arrogant and cynical young man comes to love an old man like a father even when he discovers that the old man *isn't* his father. And in the end, the hero, not a hero at all in his own life, does the heroic thing—the *right* thing. And you know what? That was enough for me to suspend my disbelief and to enjoy the movie.

Similarly, *Joe Somebody* has its issues. It is predictable. Simple. Maybe even a bit clichéd. But it is also heartwarming. The hero did the right thing, avoided violent retribution, and ended up not only with a gorgeous woman, but also with his own daughter's respect. More importantly, he ended up with *self*-respect.

Again, what is wrong with that? Why are people falling over themselves to give Oscars to violent, poorly written movies that are suffocated with special effects and astronomical acting salaries, and yet they can't see clear to recommend a couple of heartwarming little movies that espouse worthwhile values, create a few laughs, a few tears, and in the end, the desire to shout triumphantly because the hero triumphs without having to take his clothes off, kill anyone, or even cuss?

Structure? Yes. Heart? Absolutely. And to the critics who panned these movies, I say: if you were consistent enough to pan the *really* bad movies (the ones that unfortunately win awards), I'd be better able to accept your summary execution of these two flawed but fun flicks.

And my message to you writers out there? Write from the heart as well as the head. Movies without one or the other just aren't worth making or watching.

Good—and heartfelt—writing to you.

THe BiG
PiCTURE

3

14.

THE LOGLINE

Okay, so now what do you do with all these elements? Well, for one thing, you can build a "logline," a one- or two-sentence description of your script.

Loglines are used not only to pitch a project to producers, executives, or agents, but also to encapsulate the story to reveal whether it is structurally sound. There's an old saying in Hollywood: If you can't describe your story in a sentence, there's something wrong with the story. While there are obvious exceptions, when using the screenwriting formula, a short, catchy logline is your goal.

Take two extremely successful movies, *Titanic* and *Fargo*. Of the two, I believe that *Fargo* is by far the better film, an opinion supported by several "Best 100 Movie" lists that contain *Fargo* and not *Titanic*. Yet *Titanic* lends itself far better to a pitching logline: "A young couple meet and fall in love at sea ... on the maiden voyage of the *Titanic*." I don't even know how to begin pitching *Fargo*; the quality of the screenplay rests in the execution of the writing rather than its story concept.

Nonetheless, there is a certain truth to the saying that an inability to articulate the essence of your story in a line or two might indicate some structural problems. Why? Because your story is like a house—it needs to have certain elements or "building blocks." If *you* don't know what those building blocks are, a producer, agent, or executive might wonder if you bothered to *put* those building blocks into your story.

You don't get more "low concept" than *Steel Magnolias*. Great film, but not a high-concept piece (see Chapter 16) like *E.T. the Extra-Terrestrial, Jaws,* or *Titanic*. However, because it is a great film, it has those aforementioned building blocks. If you wanted to pitch the script, you'd put those elements together in a logline: "An overprotective mother is forced to choose between protecting her ailing daughter and allowing her to risk her life to have a child of her own."

Again, this might not be a high-concept piece, but knowing the elements of the story, I'm able to pitch it concisely. In a high-concept piece you don't necessarily have to know or even have all the necessary elements. Take *Jaws*, for example: "A great white shark terrorizes a tourist community." Who's the hero? Who's the opponent? What's the life-changing event? What are the enabling circumstances? Who cares? Peter Benchley made more than $5 million dollars from his rather mediocre novel simply because it had a high concept (and caught the eye of a young guy named Spielberg).

You don't need all the elements to create a pitching logline. BUT, you do need all the elements to create what I call an analytical logline. That's a logline you create not to pitch, but to analyze the structural integrity of your story.

If someone had used an analytical logline on *Titanic*, they would not have been sure of the hero, the opponent, the life-changing event, enabling circumstances, or ally. In fact, they might have noticed that the script didn't actually have a second act (or much of a third act either). However, with the help of a $250 million dollar filmmaking budget and $50 million for advertising, the filmmakers were able to create the greatest box office hit in history.

If you want to create an analytical logline, you need to include all of the necessary story elements. Those elements include all those previously mentioned: hero, flaw, enabling circumstances, opponent, ally, life-changing event, and jeopardy.

For example: When an apathetic young Gen X process server is framed for murder, he meets a compassionate woman who teaches him to care enough to not only clear his own name, but to try to stop the real killer, a terrorist with a nuclear bomb and a ticket to Disneyland. (This is the logline for one of my own screenplays, *The Server*.)

ELEMENTS OF A LOGLINE

Here is a breakdown of the analytical logline of my screenplay *The Server*.

HERO: young man

FLAW: apathy

ENABLING CIRCUMSTANCES: It's implied by the Gen X label, because it means the hero has surrounded himself with the apathy that we rightly or wrongly attribute to that generation (a generation grown old enough to have been supplanted by Gen Y). Our apathetic Gen Xer would be like Rocky Balboa in *Rocky*, a bum surrounded by bums and therefore protected from standing out. Our hero is an apathetic guy who hides in a sea of apathy.

ALLY: woman

OPPONENT: terrorist

LIFE-CHANGING EVENT: In this case, this event is our hero being framed for murder, which forces him to choose between his selfishness and a chance to do the right thing (and win the woman's heart).

JEOPARDY: He faces arrest for murder. On a larger scale, there is the possibility of a nuclear bomb being set off by the terrorist.

There are two more elements that can be applied to our list. They are inherent in our formula, but it is frequently useful to think of them as separate elements. These are the implied journey and the ally's M.O.

IMPLIED JOURNEY: The implied journey is the hero's journey to find the real murderer and to learn the compassion he needs in order to be a better man. "What is the hero's journey?" should be, and often is, a standard question asked of writers by producers and development executives. If you don't have a hero's journey, you don't have a story.

ALLY'S M.O.: Why is the ally's M.O. important? Because the ally has to be *believably* qualified to help the hero. Believable to whom? To the reader and/or viewer. If your hero is a drug addict and the ally is a Jehovah's Witness who comes to the door and wins the hero over by telling him that Jesus is "just so terribly sad" that one of his "flock" has strayed from goodness into the evil of drugs...I, for one, am not buying it.

Why? A true addict isn't going to listen to a Jehovah's Witness's sermon for more than a second, and he sure as hell isn't going to change his entire life and give up a hardcore drug addiction because of it. Who *would* be qualified to help a drug-addicted hero? How about another drug addict who has found a way to overcome the addiction? Or how about a father figure of such authority and compassion that the hero trusts his judgment? Or another drug addict who acts as a negative role model by unintentionally showing the hero where he's going to end up if he doesn't overcome his own addiction?

If you fail to convince your audience (whether in the theaters or in studio offices) that your ally can save your hero, you've lost that audience.

Importance of a Logline
It is important to include all the aforementioned elements in an analytical logline if you really want to test the structural integrity of your story.

As a development executive, I have read more than 5,000 scripts. I saw many screenplays that were missing some of these elements, and these scripts did not work for me—or for anyone else, for that matter. Remember, if you have a hole in your analytical logline, which is nothing more than an extremely short synopsis of your story, just imagine how magnified that hole will be in a 23,000-word script.

It's like aiming a gun. If the end of your barrel is an inch too far to the left, the bullet will be feet, not inches, to the left by the time it reaches the target. A bad beginning is always magnified by the time the ending comes around—of a rifle shot or a script.

One example that comes to mind is a logline submitted to me that contained no people in it. It went something like: "Nature fights back against environmental abuse." This may seem like a ridiculous example, but often the extremes best illustrate problems that exist in the norm. The author left out not one but *every* important element, including people!

Identify the Elements in Your Logline

Your job now is to identify all of the aforementioned elements in your story, and then to put them in the form of an analytical logline. At this point, don't worry how long that logline is, even if it's a "log paragraph" or a "log page."

The point is to capture and convey the essence of your story using the story's most important elements: hero, opponent, flaw, ally, life-changing event, jeopardy, enabling circumstances, implied journey, and ally's M.O. Finally, edit the extended logline until it is a short, pithy description of your story.

If you continue to have problems creating a logline that really sizzles, be patient—Chapter 16 will be of great help to you.

OBJECTIVE AND SUBJECTIVE STORYLINES

One of the ways to figure out the various elements for your logline is to look at your storylines. The original title of this book was *Two Stories to Tell*. That's because, as we discussed earlier, all well-written stories consist of two stories—the objective storyline and subjective storyline.

In *Wedding Crashers*, the objective story is whether John and Jeremy can pull off another successful wedding-crashing season without getting killed, maimed, or (even worse) romantically entangled with the wedding obsessed women they're planning to love-and-leave. The subjective storyline is whether John can finally find a meaningful romantic relationship with a woman who is worth the effort it will take to win her.

In *Million Dollar Baby*, the objective storyline is whether Frankie can train Maggie to win the women's world boxing championship. The subjective storyline is whether Frankie can redeem himself as a father figure, having failed to do so with his own daughter.

In *Leaving Las Vegas*, the objective storyline is whether Ben is actually going to drink himself to death. The subjective storyline is whether Ben can find a reason to live. They may seem to be the same thing in this case, but they're not. The objective storyline is whether a specific action is accomplished (suicide). The subjective is whether the hero can redeem himself in his own eyes enough to want to continue living.

In *Rocky*, the objective story is the story of Rocky training for and then fighting for the world heavyweight championship of the world against the current champ, Apollo Creed. The subjective storyline is the story of Rocky trying to overcome his image of being a loser. The subjective story, then, is the story of the hero becoming a better person, not just a better boxer or a better cop or a better politician. A better *person*.

In *Lethal Weapon*, the objective storyline is whether Mel Gibson's Sergeant Riggs can take down Gary Busey's bad-guy character Mr. Joshua. The subjective storyline is whether Sergeant Riggs can find a reason to go on living.

In *Hook*, the objective storyline is whether the adult Peter Pan can rescue his children from Captain Hook. By now, you should have a guess as to what the subjective storyline is—Peter Pan has to come to terms with his past and embrace his inner child.

Breaking down a screenplay into the objective and subjective storylines can help us get a better grasp of the various story elements. This simplifies the process of putting our story into a logline. A good logline also tells us what both storylines are about, so you need to make sure that you have both an objective and subjective storyline in your logline, and in your story.

Stories That Aren't Stories and Why

Okay, here's a story: A woman is sitting on a rock, looking out to sea. She's conflicted, feeling guilty about having abandoned her husband and children in order to pursue a career as a writer. As she sits on her rock, staring at the ocean, the woman works it out in her mind and comes to a resolution, deciding that she must pursue her dream and go on with her writing, even though it means that she must lose her family.

What's the subjective storyline? The woman's struggle to choose between pursuing her own interests and giving up her dream in order to care for her family. What's the objective storyline? There *is* no objective storyline. Why is this important? Because without an objective storyline there is no external story for us to see. All we see is the woman looking out to sea, maybe with a frown on her face. This woman might be going through emotional conflict and anguish as great as that of soldiers in the middle of a war, but how do we know, and why should we care? What do we see on-screen that's visually interesting? Nothing.

Okay, a cop is chasing a bad guy, finally tracks him down, and defeats him. What's the objective storyline? A cop chasing a bad guy. What's the subjective storyline? There *is* no subjective storyline. We can see spectacular special effects, gunfights, cars crashing, bombs exploding, but there is no personal, subjective story or struggle. There is no one who draws us into the story, and no one to lend a personal feel to the movie.

This last story is the Eddie Murphy movie *Metro*. The film consisted of car chases, explosions, and gunfire, but no personal, subjective story. In fact, the movie was so empty, without a subjective storyline, that halfway through they ran out of objective story. Even though Murphy's character had already caught the bad guy, the writers had to let the bad guy escape so that Murphy could do the same chase scenes all over again. There was no subjective story to reinforce and deepen the objective story.

NOTE: Most well-made stories contain *both* objective and subjective storylines.

The crucial thing to realize is that only when Frankie or John or Ben or Rocky (or any other hero) overcomes his character flaw, only when he triumphs on the *subjective* level, is he *able* to triumph on the *objective* level.

In *Wedding Crashers*, John has to overcome his fear of romantic intimacy before he can make a play for Claire. It's only when he becomes a better man on a personal level that he can attain his goal (the girl) on the objective level.

In *Million Dollar Baby*, Frankie has to overcome his fear of familial intimacy before he can train Maggie for the championship and thus give both of them the second chance they need. It's only when he becomes willing to risk himself emotionally by opening up to Maggie that he has a chance to give her the training and trust she needs to fight for the world championship.

In *Leaving Las Vegas*, Ben has to find a reason to live before he is able to give up his plan to drink himself to death. Ben has to become a better man, a man with the courage to fight for life even when it doesn't seem worth fighting for, before he has a chance to win on the objective level—to form a relationship with Sera and to go on living.

In *Rocky*, the hero has to overcome his self-definition as a loser to apply himself sufficiently to win on the objective level, going the distance against the champ.

Is every screenplay written this way? Absolutely not. There are great screenplays that break many of these rules, and if you are one of those geniuses who can toss the rules aside and write an unorthodox masterpiece like *Forrest Gump*, *Adaptation*, *Memento*, or *Donnie Darko*, then go right ahead.

If, however, you are like the rest of us, it would do you well to be aware of standard screenplay structure so that, if nothing else, you know what rules you're breaking. Breaking rules intentionally means that you're prepared for the consequences. Breaking rules that you don't even know about will leave you and your script open to a lot of surprises, not all of them happy ones.

Good Examples of Loglines

When stories have strong objective and subjective storylines, we get strong loglines.

> "A jaded, old boxing manager gets a second chance when a female fighter convinces him to train her."
>
> "A meek and alienated little boy finds a stranded extraterrestrial in his closet and has to find the courage to defy authorities to help the alien return to its home planet."
>
> "A grown-up Peter Pan, having foresworn Neverland for the 'real' world, discovers that Captain Hook has kidnapped his kids and taken them back to Neverland."
>
> "A down-and-out club fighter gets a one-in-a-million chance to fight for the championship."
>
> "A pair of sex-crazed, serial wedding crashers finally meet their female matches."

If you can't sum up the essence of your story in a sentence or two, it may be because your story has structural problems. Remember: not only does a good logline tell us what the story is about, it tells us what BOTH stories are about.

15.
THE OUTLINE

The next step after creating an analytical logline is to create an outline or a treatment of your story. An outline is exactly that—a rough outline of your script. The beginning, middle, and end, plus the other major events in your story, should all be present.

A treatment is more detailed—a brief description of every scene in your screenplay. Treatments can run as long as twenty or even fifty pages. (I've been hired to write treatments at both these lengths.) It's so detailed that you should be able to do little more than add dialogue to have a screenplay.

In Hollywood, the terms treatment and synopsis are sometimes used interchangeably. No use arguing with someone if they mean synopsis when they say treatment, but if they're asking you for either, you might want to ask them which item they actually want.

Brainstorming

Perhaps the greatest tool for turning a logline into an outline or treatment is brainstorming, which is exactly what it sounds like—you give your brain free rein to come up with ideas, scenes, dialogue, and any other facts about your story that you can think of. Then you organize these thoughts, ideas, and scenes chronologically so that they fit into your first, second, and third acts in dramatic sequence or order. You then expand those scenes, bits of dialogue, and other facts as much as you can, linking them together, using one bit to help you decide what the next bit should be.

As with everything else about storytelling, the process of brainstorming a story is one of asking and answering questions.

We know, for instance, that in our lottery story, we would use the first act to describe a hero who is from a wealthy background. We know that our hero has rebelled against her wealthy background and is now living at a much lower economic level. We know that our hero's lover is a good man, but not a financially successful one. The hero's father, the opponent, has abused his wealth and ignored his daughter, but he still wants to try to bring her back into his materialistic, greedy world.

Do you see how much we already know, just by knowing the hero, the opponent, ally, flaw, jeopardy, and life-changing event?

Start Asking Questions

Now, start asking questions.

For example, what events and conversations shown on-screen would help us understand who our hero is in this story of the woman winning the lottery? Think of ways that are both visual and entertaining to show her fear of being like her parents. Show the nature of her relationship with her lover, her tortured past as a "poor little rich girl," and so on.

We can throw in the scene in which her father comes to visit her and leaves the lottery ticket.

We can throw in a scene in which she talks either on the phone or in person with her mother to establish the relationship between them. It would help to have that relationship be a little different than her relationship with her father, otherwise you will have duplication and you might as well "pull a Disney" and kill the mother off before the story begins.

We can create a scene in which we see how much our hero genuinely loves her lover, and a scene in which we see how genuinely good-hearted, but financially unlucky, her lover (ally) is.

We can have a scene or several scenes showing our hero's friends, and how she and her lover enjoy their time with them on a very low budget, since everyone she knows is financially strapped.

We can have a scene in which the driver of a luxury car "steals" the hero's parking space, and she is disproportionately angry. Thinking of her father, she angrily claims that the other driver thinks he can act any way he wants to because he is wealthy. This would help us see her anger toward her own rich parents.

Thinking Up Scenes

Continue this process of thinking up scenes to show character, the life-changing event, the effects of the life-changing event, and the struggle, drama, and conflict it creates. As well, create or think of scenes that show the role of the opponent, the relationship between the hero and the hero's ally, and the method by which the hero's ally helps her begin to recognize and overcome her character flaw. Don't forget to show the hero's past, the opponent's point of view, and so on. You should have no shortage of scenes, given how much you have to show in act one alone.

Expand, ask questions, brainstorm, and soon you'll find that you have scene after scene, speech after speech, fact after fact, event after event, and before long you'll have a strong outline—or even a full treatment.

Plot Point Outline

Once we have brainstormed all of these scenes, they can be put into an outline. One type of outline is a plot point outline. This is a point-by-point description of the major events, realizations, defeats, victories, etc., in your story. By the way, you'll notice that the characters' names are in all caps at the first instance they are mentioned. This is a common convention that tells the reader that that particular character has entered the story for the first time. This plot point outline is about our story.

- In the middle of a battle, Ross, the leader of a squadron of elite special forces soldiers, orders a retreat that results in the death of his men, causing him to define himself as a coward.

- After the war, Ross seeks the safest job he can find, becoming an accountant for a mid-sized company. He creates a nice, safe world in which he will never be asked to do anything that might reveal his cowardice. He maintains a meek, unassuming demeanor, though he keeps his physical skills honed through rigorous exercise and participation in a weekend extreme sports group he belongs to that does rock climbing, martial arts, sky diving, etc.

- Ross is attracted to Leslie, the president of the company that he works for. Ross, however, feels too badly about himself to approach Leslie romantically.

- Leslie is attracted to Ross, but put off by his meekness.

- Matt is a company vice president who fawns on Leslie and belittles Ross.

- When asked about Matt's abuse, Ross merely states that it's his job to follow Matt's orders because Matt is his superior. Matt overhears Ross' feeble explanation, and tears into him, claiming that you take *what* you can *when* you can, because it's dog-eat-dog. Matt reveals that his father had been destroyed by "the system" and that he, Matt, will never let that happen to him.

- We see Ross' conflicting personality traits when he is asked to make the nightly bank deposit of company funds, something he's never done before. Arriving at the bank, Ross is jumped by a gang of muggers. For a few moments, Ross the accountant becomes Ross the Green Beret, and he lashes out, beating up all the muggers. However, he suddenly bolts in panic, giving in once more to his fear.

- Matt uses computers to electronically loot the company's bank accounts and investment funds. Then he disappears, leaving the company in danger of bankruptcy, and thus threatening the jobs, pensions, and life savings of the employees.

- Ross, realizing his safe world is in danger, reluctantly teams up with Leslie to track Matt down. Matt lashes out. Ross freezes in fear, nearly getting himself and Leslie killed. Only Leslie's quick thinking saves them.

- Leslie rejects Ross because he almost got them killed with his cowardice.

- Ross, humiliated, learns that Leslie has gone on alone to try to find Matt. For the first time, his cowardice is outweighed by the need to redeem himself.

- Ross catches up with Leslie and convinces her to give him another chance. She is reluctant to do so, still angry with him, especially since she does not know the real reason for his cowardice, and cannot trust him.

- To prove himself, Ross puts himself at risk to try to locate Matt, which mollifies Leslie. She bonds with Ross, who reveals a part of the reason for his cowardice.

THE OUTLINE

- Ross discovers that Leslie has her own ghosts and fears, and he is inspired by the fact that she has the courage to go on despite them.

- Ross uses Leslie as a role model to bolster his own courage, and develops stronger feelings for her.

- Ross risks himself even further to find out that Matt owns a casino/resort in the desert.

- Lacking proof of Matt's culpability, Ross and Leslie are unable to get the authorities to help them.

- Though not completely at peace with his own demons, Ross organizes the company's computer geeks/accountants into an electronic strike force to try to break into Matt's casino-based computer system to recover the money.

- Ross realizes how much is at stake for the company's other employees, and that he represents not only his own interests, and Leslie's safety, but also the interests, jobs, and life savings of every company employee. Their lives will be shattered unless the money is recovered.

- The company's computer geeks discover that it is going to be a lengthy procedure to break into the casino's computers. Thus, Ross organizes a team of fellow adrenalin junkies who jump at the chance to put their war-game skills to real use by breaking into the casino to rob it of the equivalent amount of money that Matt stole from the company.

- While the computer geeks/accountants try to break into the casino's computers, Ross leads his weekend extreme sports warriors in a break-in of Matt's casino. They skillfully bypass the casino's unusually heavy security to get into the casino's vaults.

- Ross and his men become trapped in the casino's vaults, and the casino's much heavier secondary security system locks them in.

- Ross discovers that the casino's huge vaults are actually the headquarters for a huge militia that has stolen billions of dollars and placed it in banks around the world. Unless they can get out by a certain time, Ross and his weekend warriors will be discovered and killed by Matt's casino security force.

- Matt, in order to tie up loose ends, plants a bomb in Leslie's company building, a bomb that will destroy the building and everyone in it.

- Ross learns that Matt planted the bomb in the company building, then learns that Matt has also planted a bomb in the casino, intending to kill Ross, Ross' men, Matt's security force, and the casino patrons. Matt plans to flee to Europe where he has billions of dollars hidden in various banks. Then Ross discovers proof that Leslie has been Matt's accomplice, and that Matt is double-crossing her, too.

- Matt seals off the entire casino, trapping everyone inside, and heads for the airport.

- Ross begins breaking his men out of the casino vaults, while Leslie, not knowing there is a bomb in her own building, electronically tracks Matt's escape and the money he has transferred to various bank accounts in Europe.

- Ross breaks free of the casino vaults and gets everyone out of the casino just in time to watch the casino destroyed in a massive explosion.

- Leslie finds Matt's money—all of it, not just what he's stolen from her company, and transfers it back to her own accounts.

- Leslie tracks Matt to the airport, where he is arrested.

- Ross desperately calls Leslie, who evacuates her building just in time to avoid the blast that destroys the building completely.

- Ross turns Leslie over to the police for having been Matt's accomplice.

OR: Ross embraces Leslie, having forgiven her because she helped capture Matt and return the money.

OR: Ross walks away from Leslie.

OR, it can be left ambiguous.

Is it Shakespeare? Hell, it may not even be decent *James Bond* or *Die Hard*. Nevertheless, it *is* a story, one that can be tinkered with, expanded, or changed in a number of ways. Moreover, if it's written well enough, if you execute the story outline well enough, maybe it can be a decent thriller.

I realize that what's missing from the story is an emphasis on the theme, though much of that will emerge in the actual screenplay once it's written. This should be the story of a man seeking to find a reason and an opportunity to be courageous. He finds it when he discovers that he can't run from his cowardice, nor bury it, nor lie about it, and that eventually it will catch up to him, and in the meantime he's spending his time suffering in dread anticipation. "A hero dies but once, a coward dies a thousand deaths."

This theme needs to be enunciated more clearly and strongly in this story, and in a way that is relevant to the reader/viewer. Very few of us will identify with a cowardly Green Beret. However, we can identify with a man who is afraid and who learns that he has to face those fears or suffer a fate even worse than whatever caused him to be afraid in the first place.

Breaking the Rules—or Outgrowing Them

You can break any number of rules to achieve any kind of effect you want. Of course, first you have to know what those rules are, which is what this book is for.

Will you, years from now as a great screenwriter, be following the minutiae of this formula? I hope not, because I want you to have the confidence to let your imagination run rampant. You'll use some of what's contained here, surely, even if it's only to have a hero, opponent, ally, and life-changing event. By adhering to the formula in this book, and by knowing the elements that make up that formula, you can create the foundation not just of a good story, but a good writing career.

16.
HIGH- AND LOW-CONCEPT STORIES

"High concept" is the most important phrase in Hollywood now, and has been for many years. It simply means that the premise of your story is so strong that it can be captured in one or two sentences. More importantly, it means that your story can be captured in a way that immediately "sells" it to the listener. That means, of course, that the premise has to be unique, fresh, and surprising.

If the story is high concept enough, you can seriously interest someone in it by using only the premise itself. Some examples:

> "A young couple meet and fall in love … on the maiden voyage of the *Titanic*."

> "A young boy finds a space alien in his closet and has to help it return home."

> "A dishonest lawyer is forced to tell nothing but the truth on the eve of his biggest trial."

Does a screenplay always have to be high concept? No. Some of the greatest films in history are low concept. *Steel Magnolias, Postcards from the Edge, Crash*, even *Star Wars* and *Close Encounters of the Third Kind* are fairly low-concept pieces.

Try to pitch *Star Wars* without making it sound like just another hack science fiction flick. Try to explain why a line worker from Indiana who has a close encounter with aliens is different from any number of trite heroes on the Sci-Fi channel.

However, if you have two scripts, both equally well written, I guarantee that the high-concept script will sell faster, and for more money. Of course, your story will dictate to you whether it's *Crash* or *Titanic*. But don't worry, if it's more *Steel Magnolias* or *Postcards from the Edge* than *Jurassic Park*, you'll just have to suffer through a Best Picture Oscar instead of huge box office sales. Could be worse.

A SUCCESS STORY

A great example of a high-concept story is a screenplay written by an acquaintance of mine. This writer sold the script, the first he'd ever sold, for $600,000 within a day of his agent sending it out. The premise: "A calloused radio talk show psychiatrist starts suffering the neuroses of the patients he ridicules on air, just before he's scheduled to start his own television show. He races to find a cure as he stutters, drools, and twitches his way toward his first live broadcast."

You can see this concept being played out. Imagine Adam Sandler, Chris Rock, Rob Schneider, or Will Ferrell twitching, drooling, stuttering, shoplifting, drinking, sniffing glue, shouting out obscenities at inappropriate moments, picking his nose, exposing himself in public, getting completely out of control, all while avoiding the sponsors and producers of his upcoming television show. He knows that his own callousness has caused his problems, and somehow he must confront that flaw in order to cure himself in time to do the television show.

Obviously, the only way out is to overcome his flaw of being mean-spirited toward his listeners. However, the reason this man is successful is the callousness that's gotten him into this mess in the first place. The concept is brilliant! It also features a role that top Hollywood comedic actors would kill for: Doctor Laura meets Howard Stern.

THE COMPONENTS OF HIGH CONCEPT

Let's look at the elements that are common to high-concept movies. Let's start with the high-concept story of the mean-spirited radio psychologist. It contains several crucial components that made it work to the tune of $600,000.

First, it has a definite profession for the hero: radio psychologist. Note that it could just as well have been a situation rather than a profession. For example, in *Liar Liar*, Jim Carrey's profession as a lawyer is integral to the storyline. However, his profession as a banker is irrelevant to the storyline in *The Mask*. What makes *The Mask* high concept and an extremely funny and successful movie is the situation: A meek nobody finds a mask that turns him into the ancient, wild-eyed god of mischief.

Second, the story gives the hero a very definite flaw that is related to his profession. Being unsympathetic certainly causes problems and goes against the usual image of a psychologist. Being unsympathetic does not go either with or against the usual image of a plumber or pianist or janitor.

Third, an event forces the character to choose between his flaw and some opportunity. In the case of this story, it's the opportunity for the hero (the radio psychologist) to overcome his newly acquired neuroses and to learn how to be empathetic to his radio patients.

Fourth, the idea is fresh. I've never heard this particular story before or since.

Fifth, there is a strong sense of irony at play. It is extremely ironic that a psychologist starts exhibiting the neurotic behavior of his patients. It would not be ironic for a plumber or baker to start exhibiting the neurotic behaviors of their customers.

A psychologist who unwillingly adopts the neuroses of his patients is funny. It's also very useful in terms of story. It forces the psychologist to confront his flaw. It also causes him to understand how painful those neuroses are, especially given that he has created a successful radio show by making fun of both the neuroses and the people who suffer them. He's made a career out of being a jerk, and his newly acquired neuroses bring that point home to him.

The Problem Must Relate to
Both the Hero's Flaw and to Who He Is

What's really important here? That the problem relates to both the hero's flaw and to who he is. If the hero in this story were a dog groomer, it wouldn't be as effective. A story about a dog groomer who takes on the neuroses of his clients doesn't make sense and doesn't make anyone laugh.

If the hero had been an empathetic, caring psychologist, it wouldn't have been as effective either. There wouldn't be as strong a sense of irony or any connection to the hero's flaw. There's no irony arising from a caring psychologist who for no reason starts taking on the neuroses of the patients he's trying so hard to help. It might still be funny, but that humor is going to be undercut by the unfairness of a nice guy suffering humiliation and the possible ruin of his career. As well, if the psychologist is a nice guy, the only way for him to redeem himself is eliminated. If he's a nice guy who suffers this calamity for no apparent reason, what does he do to get over it? We have the following components of a high-concept story:

- A hero with a definite profession or situation in life

- A hero with a definite flaw that's related to his profession and/or situation

- An event that forces the main character to choose between his flaw and some opportunity related to his flaw and to his profession and/or situation

- A sense of irony arising from the relationship between the event and the hero's profession or situation

---

THE HOOK

A character who is intrinsically conflicted is also most likely intrinsically interesting. Another name for this is *the hook*. A literary hook is any device that spices up a character, situation, or scene by adding intrinsic conflict or intrinsic comedy.

Peter Pan is a nice little story, but how do you add a hook (no pun intended) to give it a fresh feel? I mean, we've already seen Mary Martin and Cathy Rigby, right?

How about a grown-up Peter Pan who's forgotten who he is until his children are kidnapped by Captain Hook? This is the basis for Steven Spielberg's smash hit, *Hook*.

How about the story of a man who is a mathematical genius? Boring. However, what if the mathematical genius is an idiot savant whose lowlife brother wants to use him to break the bank in Vegas?

This, of course, is the Oscar-winning *Rain Man*.

What about a mathematical genius who works as a janitor at MIT? This is the Oscar-winning *Good Will Hunting*.

What about a schizophrenic mathematical genius who may or may not be a spy? That's the Oscar-winning *A Beautiful Mind*.

A movie about a mathematical genius might not fly, unless there is some hook that creates a natural conflict in the mathematical genius—and creates at least three Academy Awards!

Hooks can be applied to situations as well as characters. For instance, two enemy soldiers go to war for their respective countries. The hook? The warring countries have agreed that instead of having an all-out war, they will place only two warriors on an island to battle it out. Whichever soldier wins will win the "war" for his country.

Darren McGavin starred in a television movie in 1970 entitled *The Challenge* using this hook. An additional hook was also used—both countries sneak one additional soldier onto the island as an insurance policy. McGavin ends up battling not only the opposing country's soldier and the opposing country's extra soldier, but his own country's additional soldier as well, because the additional soldier has to kill McGavin to prevent him from revealing that his country cheated.

Decades after first watching this television movie, I still remember it because of the hooks the writers used.

Using hooks is the way to make your piece high concept. This means you take an unusual, fresh approach to a subject, one you can describe in one sentence that captures the imagination and interest of a producer or studio executive.

CAN WE CREATE HIGH-CONCEPT STORIES ON DEMAND?

The important question is: can we quantify high concept? Can we come up with principles that help us create high-concept stories on demand?

Applying the Components

Let's try to apply these components and see if we can come up with a high-concept story right here and now. Let's pick a hero with a specific flaw that relates to who he is and/or what he does. Then we'll find a problem that relates directly to who he is and to his flaw, and that forces him to confront that flaw.

Let's be random about this, just as an experiment. Let's go with the dog groomer we've already mentioned. Why? Because I've already said he's not a good candidate for a high-concept story, and I love a challenge.

To start, we need an event that relates to both his profession and to his flaw. Let's say that he becomes a dog himself. Okay, at least it's relevant to what he does. Now we need to find a flaw that's relevant to both who and what he is, and to the event.

Let's say that the dog groomer has a lot going for him but he doesn't realize it. In fact, he's quite bitter and jealous about not being more successful. He feels as if the dogs he grooms have a better life than he does. One day he states that he'd rather be one of his wealthy clients' pets than a lowly dog groomer.

SHAZAAM!! Our hero trades places with a wealthy client's horny male dog.

Now is this high concept? Can we state it clearly in a sentence or two? An unappreciative dog groomer accidentally change places with one of his rich clients' pampered pets—a horny but infertile pit bull who's facing castration unless he can impregnate a champion female pit bull.

The pit bull in the groomer's body eats raw meat, relieves himself in public, and humps sofas, dogs, and every girl he can catch. He does get into trouble, however, when he tries to hump a 180-pound Mastiff.

Meanwhile, the groomer faces either bestiality or castration unless he can find a way back to his suddenly attractive human life.

Funny? Yes. Good comic potential? Yes. However, it's not as good as the story about the psychologist. Why? Primarily because it's not unique. *The Shaggy D.A.* comes to mind. Too much like Tim Allen's remake of *The Shaggy Dog* as well. There are many other examples of stories that make this one seem just too familiar. It's been done too many times. It's not unique and it's not fresh.

Does that mean this concept isn't viable? No. It just means that it's not as high concept as my friend's script. And it might be worth noting that Disney was panned for depending on this kind of fare: remakes of outdated movies such as *The Shaggy Dog*, *The Absent Minded Professor*, and *The Love Bug* series.

ANOTHER HIGH-CONCEPT EXAMPLE

Try this: The President of the United States is infected with a germ warfare agent that forces him to tell the truth—and he's contagious!

This is the concept for *Truthies*, a script I wrote years before *Bulworth*, *Dave*, or *Liar Liar* were released. However, for some reason, I didn't get around to pitching it, and Hollywood caught up to me—several times. *Truthies*, like the radio psychologist story, is so easily conveyed in a single line that it is extremely high concept. Unfortunately, it is no longer fresh or unique.

Truthies highlights the other problems with our hypothetical dog groomer story. For one thing, the relationship between the flaw and the profession is not strong enough. Politicians and lawyers lie, therefore it's funny and ironic when one is forced to tell the truth. Psychologists cure their patients, so it's funny that instead of making his patients sane, a shrink's patients make *him* crazy. What does a dog groomer do? He grooms dogs. Being envious does not connect as strongly or naturally to a dog groomer as lying does to a politician.

There is also, by the way, something at least a little unlikable about the professions used in the radio psychologist story and in *Truthies*: There is a know-it-all, manipulative, egghead shrink who wants to dissect us; and also a lying, manipulative politician.

In fact, *Liar Liar* worked precisely *because* of the hero's profession. Jim Carrey's character, Fletcher Reede, was worse than a politician; he was a *lawyer*! Imagine a lying, weaselly lawyer forced to tell the truth. Imagine a cold-hearted, arrogant psychologist suffering the symptoms of the poor people whose lives he holds in his uncaring hands. Not just irony, but a *fitting* irony.

What do we have against dog groomers? What strong characteristics, either positive or negative, do we associate with dog groomers? None, I suspect. Does this make it impossible for us to write a story about a dog groomer? No, but if I'm looking for a one-sentence description of a story high-concept enough to snag an executive/producer/agent's attention, "A dog groomer becomes a dog," doesn't do it.

So why does "A psychologist begins taking on his patient's symptoms" make it? Because we can immediately imagine the consequences in specific terms. "The President of the United States is infected with a virus that forces him to tell the truth—and he's contagious." This immediately brings to mind implications, problems, scenes, dialogue, humor, drama, and irony.

There's that word again: irony. This is a big part of it. So is conflict. It may not be *humorously* ironic that a priest fall in love with a woman, as happened in the hit miniseries and novel *The Thorn Birds*, but it is still ironic and filled with conflict and drama. "A priest falls in love" is all you need to imagine all sorts of scenes, problems, and conflicts. Why? Because the job description entails responsibilities that *directly* conflict with the event—and the flaw.

A priest is charged with caring for the spiritual needs of those around him, in a fatherly, asexually loving way. Falling in love and having an affair runs directly counter to that responsibility and image.

A psychologist is charged with curing neuroses. Adopting the neuroses of his patients directly conflicts with the psychologist's supposed responsibilities.

We have come to regard lawyers and politicians as the ultimate liars. To have either of these professions forced to tell the truth runs counter to the qualities we ascribe to them. There is intrinsic conflict. What does a lawyer do if he can't lie when representing a client that he knows is guilty? What does a politician do if he starts to tell all of the dirty government secrets?

This is the most powerful element or quality of a high-concept logline: It is immediately evocative of what the story is about.

This is still not enough, though. Why? If the concept has been done before you will have trouble selling it.

Although *Truthies* is extremely high concept, I waited too long to pitch it to executives and agents. *Dave, Liar Liar,* and *Bulworth* put *Truthies* in its grave. Suddenly "The President is infected with virus that forces him to tell the truth" is no longer evocative of something *unique*, but evokes other movies that are too similar for *Truthies* to be commercially viable. Time may sometimes cure the "that reminds me of that other movie" problem, and I have, in fact, recently started getting interest in *Truthies.* It even placed well in a major competition, indicating that perhaps enough time has passed that it is once again fresh enough to be considered high concept. Time will tell.

WHAT WE HAVE SO FAR

What do we have so far in our search for a formula for creating high-concept loglines?

a) We need a hero whose job, profession, or situation in life involves strong responsibilities or qualities (either positive or negative) that are "public knowledge." For example, the public doesn't attribute any particular qualities to a dog groomer, but we do attribute very definite qualities to politicians and lawyers.

b) We need an event that runs counter to those responsibilities or qualities in a strong, dramatic, and original way. For example, a lawyer or a politician always telling the truth, or a priest falling in love.

c) We need the conflict between the event and the hero's qualities/profession to be strongly evocative of specific scenes, images, dialogue, problems, and so on. We immediately see the problems that a smitten priest will face.

MeMoRaBLe QUoTeS

"I have always depended on the kindness of strangers."

—A STREETCAR NAMED DESIRE

"Hasta la vista, baby."

—TERMINATOR 2: JUDGMENT DAY

Striker: *"Surely you can't be serious."*

Rumack: *"I am serious... and don't call me Shirley."*

—AIRPLANE!

"Oh, no, it wasn't the airplanes. It was Beauty killed the Beast."

—KING KONG

d) We need the event to be something unfamiliar and unexpected. A priest telling the truth is not unfamiliar or unexpected. A priest falling in love is, and has all sorts of interesting and dramatic implications for the hero.

Begin With the Hero

Let's begin with a hero who has a profession or situation that carries responsibilities and qualities strongly ascribed to it by the public.

How about a priest who is asked by the devil to represent him in a lawsuit against God?

I know I jumped a step or two there, but I had to go with the inspiration. If we had been a little more methodical, we would have first decided upon a profession, such as priest. We then could have mulled over what kind of events would run counter to the responsibilities and/or reputation of a priest. *The Thorn Birds* was about a priest falling in love with a woman, which certainly is high concept, counter to what we expect of priests. What else runs counter to what we normally think of as a priest's responsibilities or reputation? A priest serves God. What if a priest was forced to serve Satan instead of God?

How you answer that question is going to depend on your particular imaginative bent. My own "flash" was in terms of the added oddity of a priest who was a lawyer. There are priests who are also lawyers. Even so, the combination of lawyer and priest will probably seem funny to the public, because it certainly has conflict built into the job description!

The Middle Acts and the Hero's Flaw

We're still missing something here—the middle acts. When I said that high concept is evocative of scenes, ideas, dialogue, I was really saying that the logline would be evocative of the second and third acts. I say that because most loglines are actually descriptions of the first act: "A couple meets and falls in love on the maiden voyage of the Titanic." "A little boy finds a space alien in his closet." "A former WWII American patriot embittered by the loss of his lover encounters her, and she asks him to save her war-hero husband."

So far, with this Priest/Devil logline, there is no second or third act.

We're also missing the hero's flaw. This is crucial, because unless the priest has some kind of flaw, the story is over before it starts. What priest is going to represent the Devil in *any* matter, much less in a lawsuit against *God?* Unless, of course...there is some flaw that drives him to do it.

Jim Carrey's character in *Liar Liar* was a liar, which is the only reason that forcing him to tell the truth is effective. It was his flaw (lying) that made telling the truth interesting—and filled with conflict. Similarly, unless our lawyer/priest has a flaw, his representing the devil is not enough—and not believable. So, let's create a flaw for our priestly hero.

Maybe the priest is having a crisis of faith. Perhaps he's fallen in love, or perhaps he's been witness to a tragedy that's caused him to question the goodness of God. Maybe a friend, family member, or other loved one has died of cancer or some other illness or accident. Therefore, our hero's flaw is a lack of faith, appropriately ironic in a priest.

Our High-Concept Logline

Okay, here's our logline: A darkly irreverent comedy in which a priest, driven to a crisis in faith by the suffering of the world, agrees to represent the Devil in a class action lawsuit against God.

Hm. Not bad. So yes, I believe we can quantify high concept and create high-concept stories by using the components we've discussed in this chapter. I just did. Now it's your turn!

As I mentioned earlier, your screenplay doesn't have to be high concept. Some of the best movies ever made are not particularly high concept. *Forrest Gump* defies a logline. *Casablanca* is hard to pitch in just a line or two. *The Trip to Bountiful*, *Driving Miss Daisy*, *Fargo*, *Steel Magnolias*, and *Postcards from the Edge* are all low-concept movies, all of them brilliant. However, high concept does make it easier to get a script read, especially for a newcomer.

It's like having a photo of that remote cabin you're trying to sell. If the potential buyer likes what he sees in the photo, he might be willing to travel to see the cabin itself. Similarly, if you can have a "photo" that captures the essence of the story in an interesting way, it might be attractive enough to entice an executive or agent into reading the actual script.

CAN WE TURN LOW CONCEPT INTO HIGH CONCEPT?

Can we use our new high-concept formula to turn a low-concept script into a high-concept script? Let's find out.

I wrote a screenplay called *The Server*. It was meant to be a big action piece, totally commercial. *The Server* is about an

---

apathetic Gen-X process server who only serves delinquent baby boomer dads, because his own father abandoned him when he was a child. A process server is, of course, someone who is paid to find people and serve them with papers, such as subpoenas, divorce papers, summons, et al.

One day, someone anonymously hires our uncaring hero to locate a particularly hard-to-find delinquent dad. Our hero finds the man in the company of two other men who are obviously cops of some kind. As our hero tries to serve the man, shots ring out, and the man and his two police companions fall dead.

Our hero escapes, along with a beautiful female by-stander. Both our hero and the breathtaking bystander are then framed for the murders by the real killer—a terrorist who used our hero to find a member of his group who was about to tell the FBI about the terrorist leader's plan to set off a huge bomb in Los Angeles.

You can see the problem right away, I'm sure: It took me a paragraph to describe the concept, and even an entire paragraph didn't create any real excitement, surprise, or humor.

Let's see if we can change it so that you can understand the method to create your own high-concept story. Then you can apply the method to either a new script, or to a script you have already written but that you haven't been able to sell. Let's go through the high-concept process again, systematically.

First, we need a hero whose profession, situation, and/or reputation carries a lot of dramatic responsibilities and/or qualities known and accepted by the public. Who is our hero? A process server. What responsibilities and/or qualities do the general public associate with that profession? None, unfortunately. This is our first roadblock. However, our hero is a Gen-Xer slacker, and we do associate certain qualities with that designation, namely laziness, anti-establishmentarianism, irresponsibility—they are the MTV Generation.

Next, we need a character flaw that runs counter to the responsibilities or qualities associated with the hero. What is our hero's character flaw? Bitterness over his father having abandoned him. Here's another problem—this character flaw does not run counter to the qualities and/or responsibilities of his position or situation.

The fact that we're encountering problems is great! Why? Because we see how useful this formula is as an analytical tool, allowing us to spot the weaknesses in our story.

So, our hero's flaw, (bitterness), doesn't run counter to what we expect of a slacker. Of course, the hero's going to be bitter—that's part of his job description as a Gen-Xer. So the flaw doesn't work.

When I wrote *The Server*, I had analyzed more than 5,000 scripts, rewritten scripts for production companies and studios, and had written half a dozen of my own screenplays, yet I still made a fundamental error with *The Server*. However, the important point is that our high- concept formula allowed me to finally understand that error. Our high-concept formula works as an analytical tool.

How would I, as a script doctor, "fix" *The Server*? Well, if someone came to me with a hero who is an apathetic, irreverent Gen-Xer, I would put that slacker into the most unlikely position possible to create an instant conflict. I might, for instance, have him inherit a relative's huge business, and then be forced to try to run it in order to avoid having the business and its employees go under. A slacker trying to run a Fortune 500 company is funny and high concept.

A slacker trying to track down a terrorist is not high concept enough to generate excitement. The fact that the hero is a slacker is not necessary to the story. It's the story of someone trying to stop a terrorist from blowing up Los Angeles. Who that someone is is irrelevant. I broke another of the "rules" of high concept: The hero's position or profession isn't related to either the event or the flaw. By using our high-concept formula, we have been able to quickly and accurately determine what was wrong with my script. It also gave me a great idea for that next script: "A Gen X 'slacker' inherits a business that he has to learn how to run."

However, let's not digress from our primary purpose in this section: to turn the low-concept *The Server* into a high-concept piece.

Two Approaches

There are two possible approaches to making *The Server* more high concept: We can change the life-changing event, or we can change the hero and his flaw.

Given the same hero, a rebellious, anti-establishment, irresponsible slacker, the strongest kind of life-changing event would be one which would force him to choose between his flawed lifestyle and some opportunity.

Let's say our slacker hero falls in love with a woman who is wealthy, educated, and refined. Our hero comes to believe that the only way he can win that woman is to become like her: wealthy, erudite, and classy. Now our hero has to choose between his anti-establishmentarianism and the opportunity of being with the woman he's fallen in love with—a woman whose wealth and position symbolize the very establishment he's spent his life bucking.

This could be a nice romantic comedy, and a fairly high-concept movie that can be clearly stated in a sentence or two: "A rebellious Gen Xer falls in love with a beautiful upperclass woman and decides he must become as refined and successful as she is in order to win her love."

This actually works rather nicely. The concepts are extremely easy to state. It could be either a low-budget film like *When Harry Met Sally* or a star-driven romantic comedy like *You've Got Mail*.

The problem is that there is nothing left of the original *The Server*. That's okay, except that what we're doing isn't fixing *The Server*, but rather taking one single element from it to write an entirely different script. Well, if the new script sells, we'll never give a damn about the original *Server* still being flawed!

However, let's see if we can keep the life-changing event, but change the hero to make *The Server* work.

The life-changing event is our hero being framed for murder. Okay, so what's the problem? The problem is that the life-changing event itself has been done a million times. Hundreds, maybe thousands of movies have been written around a hero being framed for murder.

Killer Popes, Alien Overlords, and Old Ladies, Oh My!

Is there any way of making the hero so unusual that it becomes high concept for him to be framed for murder? Yes. The Pope is framed for murder. The alien ambassador from another planet is framed for murder. A ninety-year-old great grandmother is framed for murder. Are these high concepts? Not yet. We have still to connect the three components of high concept: hero's profession/situation, flaw, and life-changing event.

If the Pope is framed for murder, how does being framed for murder relate to either his profession or to his flaw? Let's fill in the blanks. The Pope, corrupted by the power and prestige of his position, is framed for the murder of a former mistress by an ambitious bishop. He must find a way to clear his name without destroying the church.

The ambassador from the first extraterrestrial race to contact Earth is framed for murder by a right-wing religious leader. The alien diplomat must survive long enough to convince a panicked planet Earth that he is not the vanguard of a murderous alien invasion.

A bitter, wealthy, self-pitying old woman stuck in a nursing home by her uncaring family decides to leave her fortune to a pet shelter. She is then framed for murder by a relative trying to take control of her estate. She must prove her innocence while fleeing from the police, the tabloid press, and her own murderous relatives.

These loglines are off the top of my head. I'm sure that by using the high-concept formula and other tools in this book, they can be honed to an even higher level.

Are they evocative? Certainly. I can see scenes in which the wheelchair-bound old lady uses her wits to flee the police, then befriends a young tabloid journalist who's hounding her for an interview. In the process, she becomes a national cause célèbre.

I can see the Pope, all pomp and ceremony, forced to suddenly take stock of his life and the questionable decisions he has made as a member of the church hierarchy: his WWII collaboration with the Nazis in order to avoid harm to the Church, perhaps an affair or two, and the fact that the bishop who wants to kill him has a valid point—the Pope is making a mockery of the Church and threatening to destroy it.

This story is essentially that of a good man who has misplaced his goodness and must find it again so that he can do the right thing. Meanwhile, he tries to figure out how to save the Church from being destroyed by a scandal, and himself from the bishop's murderous intentions. What if the woman whose death the Pope is being blamed for is the wrong woman? She was a *friend* of his former lover, and as the philandering Pope flees the bishop's killers, he turns for help to the woman who really *was* his lover so many years before.

THE FORMULA WORKS!

These loglines are roughhewn because they're still dripping ink from the presses, but they are good, high-concept premises.

The formula allows us to analyze our stories to see if the concepts are solid; it allows us to create high concepts and to build our stories around those concepts; it helps us to determine if our concepts are sound enough to be worth pursuing; and it allows us to see the weaknesses before we commit to writing a doomed script.

17. A TiTaNiC UNDERTaKING

I can hear you now: "Is he nuts? He wants to fix the most successful script ever written?" Yes, because it desperately needs fixing.

In fact, *Titanic* (James Cameron's version, not Charles Bracket's earlier and much better version) succeeded *in spite of* an extremely weak script. The Academy of Motion Picture Arts and Sciences recognized this by giving *Titanic* just about every one of its awards, but withholding even a nomination for best screenplay. None of the actors won Oscars because of the weak writing. You can act your heart out, but if the writing is weak, your dialogue and character will be weak.

How does a film win for Best Picture without even being *nominated* for best screenplay? It wins by beating the public into submission with $250 million dollars of special effects, the biggest advertising budget in history, and the biggest opening (most number of theaters) of any film in history.

Now remember, making even a bad film takes a Herculean amount of effort, and I admire anyone who does it. In addition, James Cameron, who was born and grew up a few miles from my own home town in Northern Ontario, Canada, has written and directed some outstanding films, such as the first two *Terminator* films, among the very best action films ever made, as well as *Aliens, Rambo: First Blood, Part II*, and *The Abyss*, all box office smashes.

But *Titanic?* Well... not so much.

Now you may not believe me, and that's okay. But after the euphoria of *Titanic* faded away, more and more movie industry experts came forward and admitted that the "greatest movie of all time" was actually not that great in retrospect.

Time Magazine has an extremely well respected top 100 films list. No *Titanic*.

The International Movie Data Base (www.imdb.com) is an invaluable site for writers and lists the top 250 movies. No *Titanic*.

The American Film Institute has a top 100 films list that is perhaps the *most* respected in the country. You guessed it: no *Titanic*.

This is not to slam Mr. Cameron, a veteran and extremely successful writer/director and, by his own words, "King of the world." It is rather to point out that even *Titanic*, the most financially successful film of all time, can stand some fixing. So "fix" it I will.

USING THE TOOLS

Let's look at the three main story elements of *Titanic*: the hero and his position or profession; the life-changing event; and the hero's flaw.

Who is the hero of *Titanic*? It's actually unclear; it's either Leonardo DiCaprio's character Jack, or Kate Winslet's character Rose. This makes it difficult to figure out the flaw, but let's say for the sake of argument that the hero is Rose.

Her flaw? Well, here we have another problem, because she is *loaded* with flaws. She is spoiled, moody, immature, whiny, and rebellious. And she allows her mother to talk her into marrying a man for money rather than love, so there's some kind of flaw there, I suppose (prostitution comes to mind). However, from the very beginning, Rose defies her mother, making it clear that she doesn't want to marry the rich man. She does everything she can to sabotage the marriage, lacking the maturity or consideration to be honest with her fiancé. She sneaks around behind his back, embarrassing him, rather than having the courage to tell him the truth.

Now, pick a flaw. Why does having more than one major flaw pose a problem? Because in a well-written screenplay, the hero's flaw forms the basis for the story. How the hero corrects that flaw or falls fatal victim to it *is* the story. It takes an entire screenplay to tell it. So, what happens when you have, say, five major flaws, as does Rose? You either do not adequately address or resolve all of them, or you have a ten-hour movie in which you try to deal with all the storylines created by them. This is the reason that the screenplay did not receive critical acclaim, although the film itself did: several of the major story elements are unclear, including who the hero is, and what the flaw is.

That gives us at least two things that need to be fixed: the hero and the flaw. Let's go on to the third major element of high concept: the life-changing event that forces the hero to choose between her flaw and an opportunity.

There are really only two major events in the film. Rose falls in love with Jack, and the ship sinks.

The sinking of the ship doesn't happen until far too late in the film to be an effective life-changing event. Also, because it's unclear what her flaw is, it's difficult to know how either the sinking of the ship or falling in love with Jack can force Rose to choose between her flaw and some opportunity. It's also unclear what that opportunity *is*.

However, there is an element of high concept to this script. Two lovers fall in love on the maiden voyage of the *Titanic*. It's strong, even though it lacks a second or third act. So, let's use our formula to create a stronger hero, flaw, and act one event.

We've already made Rose the hero. Her flaw? Let's make it that she's given up on her one true love in order to marry for money. Let's make it *her* decision to marry for money (rather than her mother's). We'll be clear that it's her flaw, not her mother's. Instead of trying to sabotage her engagement to her fiancé, she does everything she can to convert it into an actual wedding so that she can be the rich lady of the house rather than the impoverished spouse of an Irish potato farmer.

Who's the opponent? It can be the fiancé, I suppose. Alternatively, it could be a story in which the opponent and the hero's ally are the same person, which often happens in love stories, such as *When Harry Met Sally*.

So let's make Jack both the opponent and the hero's ally. He opposes the hero's desire to sell herself to her rich fiancé. He is also the one person best suited to helping her to overcome her flaw, which is greed, born of desperation and poverty.

Now, another problem with *Titanic* is that the romance between the two callow youths happens far too quickly to be believable, especially given their lack of maturity and experience. Let's fix that too. Let's say that Rose is a tad bit older, perhaps mid-to-late twenties. She's engaged to a wealthy American. They board the *Titanic*, the rich fiancé intending to bring her home to an American wedding.

As they board the ship, Rose sees the lower-class passengers, many of them Irish, being herded aboard like cattle, and she feels upset and guilty. Then she sees him: a man her own age, a tall, ruggedly handsome Irishman. It's the lover she had abandoned for her rich fiancé. He is the man she truly loves—with her heart, rather than with her purse. Now the stage is set. The passion between Rose and her lover already exists, so we don't have to worry about the glaring fact that a few days aboard ship isn't enough time to develop a believable romance of any depth, especially not a life-or-death love.

The conflict, then, is between Rose's passion and her greed.

The other conflict is also already established: In our new *Titanic*, Rose isn't from a family that has fallen on hard times, but rather from a lower class family like that of her lover's.

Our hero has consciously chosen to abandon her class and the people in it, including her lover. However, here comes the lover, representing not only the love she's abandoned, but also the people, country, and economic and social class she's rejected in favor of wealth gotten under false pretenses—she does not love the man offering that wealth.

Now *Titanic* (the ship) actually has relevance. You see, in the current *Titanic*, the ship has nothing to do with anything. The sinking takes place far too late to be an effective act one event. Neither of the main characters has anything to do with the ship, nor does the hero's flaw. However, if the hero's flaw is clearly greed, which has led her to abandon her own people, and she boards a ship that is the ultimate symbol of twentieth-century greed in the face of worldwide poverty, then there is a very strong connection between her flaw, the ship, and her lover. The ship becomes a symbol.

What is the life-changing event? The event is discovering that her lover is aboard the ship. Why? Because this event will force her to choose between her greed and the opportunity of being with the man she really loves. And the background is now quite powerful: She has thrown her lot in with the rich and powerful and sits on the top decks of the most luxurious ship in the world, while the poor passengers, including her own lover, huddle miserably below decks.

This is a contrast and conflict Mr. Cameron created, and it's a damned good one. The problem is that Rose makes her choice too early and too easily, jetting down below decks to dance and party with Jack and the poor people in steerage.

In our script, the choice is never easy. She fights to retain her flaw, because she believes her life depends on that flaw. She believes that marrying a rich American will save her life, or at least save her from a life of hardship on, the rocky, moss-covered farms of the Emerald Isle. Every minute of the movie becomes Rose's conscious choice to abandon her lover, her people, her country, and her heart.

Every minute that Rose sees her lover among the cattle-like lower-class passengers, while she wears beautiful clothes and hobnobs with beautiful people, every minute becomes an indictment and a challenge to her. Seeing her lover among the disadvantaged and poorly-treated passengers forces Rose to choose repeatedly between the luxury symbolized by the *Titanic's* first class, and the opportunity of being below decks with the only man she loves.

Now that Rose's lover is someone she's already felt deeply for, it's more believable that she would be this much in love. It is also more believable that she would feel torn between her lover and the chance of being a millionaire's wife. I mean, let's face it, why the heck would Rose choose a punky, dirt poor kid whose main accomplishment is spitting, rather than the rich, good-looking social superstar Cal, played by Billy Zane?

In our new version, when Rose finally chooses, it's between a deep love and a deep greed, rather than between a life of luxury and a life with an uncultured street urchin. In our version, the struggle is also between Rose's past and future, her people and her own selfish desires, the abandonment of her culture, her country, her family, and her lover.

In James Cameron's *Titanic*, Rose seems like an idiot for throwing away a lifetime of wealth for a fling with someone she doesn't even know, someone with absolutely nothing to offer her, financially or emotionally. In Mr. Cameron's story, Jack isn't old enough or mature enough to offer real, romantic love. He's essentially an irresponsible, uncultured street urchin, and their life together is bound to be an unhappy, poverty-ridden failure.

However, our story has an older Jack, one with whom Rose already has a substantial history and a substantial love. Even more, that love represents Rose's people, her country, and even her own family. Now she has a tremendous amount to lose by being with the rich guy, and the whole story makes more sense, especially if she ends up choosing her poor lover over her rich fiancé.

Contrast that decision with the choice between the rich, handsome, famous fiancé and the poor, semi-literate, loogie-hawking street scammer.

Our story becomes that of an ambitious (and/or desperate?) young Irish woman who abandons her one true love, as well as her family, country, and heritage, to marry for money. She boards a luxury liner with her rich fiancé, headed for an American wedding, only to discover that her lover has followed her aboard...on the maiden voyage of the *Titanic*.

Compare that to Mr. Cameron's version: A callow young woman who is engaged to a handsome, wealthy man she does not love takes up with a young street urchin who teaches her to spit and have sex in the back seat of a car on the maiden voyage of the *Titanic*.

Look at how disjointed the elements are in the produced version of *Titanic*. See how weak the logline is?

What's the life-changing event? What's the hero's flaw? Who *is* the hero? How do the elements relate to each other, *cause* each other, *arise* from each other, *magnify* each other? In Mr. Cameron's version, the elements don't do any of these things.

Here's my *Titanic* test: Quote one memorable line from the movie. Here is the only response I've ever gotten to that question: "I'm the king of the world!" I always smile calmly when I hear that response. Usually so does the speaker, often blushing.

I can quote you a *dozen* great lines from *Casablanca* off the top of my head. *Gone With the Wind, Forrest Gump, Steel Magnolias, Postcards from the Edge, Good Will Hunting,* and *As Good as It Gets* all have great lines associated with them. It's not just because the dialogue was better written (it certainly was). Those are films whose elements meshed and reinforced each other, creating stronger, more unique characters, more interesting situations for those characters, and more memorable dialogue for the actors.

Look at the sidebars throughout this book for some of the most memorable Hollywood quotes. Not a bad movie in the bunch. In fact, probably not a line of dialogue that doesn't instantly identify the film it came from and the character who spoke it. Remember: Dialogue arises out of structure and the interaction of the story elements. So too do characterization, theme, drama, and conflict.

THIS IS WHAT THIS BOOK IS ABOUT

That, in the end, is what this book is about. Would I like to be receiving the writer's residuals from *Titanic*? You betcha', and if I were James Cameron I wouldn't care what some schmuck like Rob Tobin said about the quality of the *Titanic* script.

However, *as* that schmuck Rob Tobin, what I *really* want is to help you learn how to be able to write screenplays that not only sell, but that make me cry, make me fall in love, make me examine my own life, and make me want to shout in triumph, joy, anger, fear, surprise, or indignation.

My heart broke as Forrest Gump stood over his lover's grave, after she finally came home to him, but too late.

I felt afraid when Tom Hanks, in *Big*, huddled in a cheap motel room, a little boy having awoken in a man's body.

I felt for the characters in *Steel Magnolias* and also felt the victory in Sally Fields' affirmation that she wouldn't have missed a moment of being a mother to her now dead daughter.

I laughed through *Airplane!*, *Blazing Saddles*, *Young Frankenstein*, and *Being There*.

And, though I saw the gaping holes in the second and third acts of *Saving Private Ryan*, I recognized that Spielberg's first half hour of raw, shocking war footage would make that film important.

This is what I want: for brilliant screenplays to be written, screenplays that make a difference to the world, regardless of who writes them. And if this book helps *one* of you write one *Forrest Gump*, *Good Will Hunting*, *As Good as It Gets*, or *Casablanca*, then it will stand as one of my life's most precious achievements.

Write your hearts out, and write your hearts *in*—*into* your stories, characters, dialogue, and theme. And follow the formula that has led to the making of the greatest films of all time:

Casablanca
As Good as It Gets
Good Will Hunting
Secrets and Lies
The Lord of the Rings
Forrest Gump
Steel Magnolias
Big
Raiders of the Lost Ark
Star Wars
Back to the Future
Close Encounters
Saving Private Ryan
Memento
Donnie Darko
The Big Chill
Fargo
Heaven Can Wait
Postcards from the Edge
The Princess Bride
Airplane!
Blazing Saddles
The Terminator

… 'nuff said.

APPENDIX A: PREWRITING TECHNIQUES

This appendix contains techniques you can use before you sit down to actually write your screenplay. These are meant to get your juices flowing, so you don't have to start writing when your pen and paper—or computer screen and keyboard—are cold. These techniques are also useful for overcoming writer's block.

PREWRITING TECHNIQUE #1: FOCUSED FREEWRITING

Focused freewriting involves sitting down with pen or keyboard in hand, topic in mind, and beginning to write. The only rules are to stay on topic as much as possible, and to not stop writing, *no matter what*—not even for a *second*. If you have to write nonsense, like "who the hell is this Tobin guy anyway, and what makes him think that this will help me with my article on nudity among Patagonian Indians?" then do it, and come back to the topic as soon as you can.

Just don't stop writing!

What follows is a snippet from a freewriting session. The passage is unedited, complete with the original typos, save for the deletion of a few colorful expletives:

Okay, here we go: I'm sitting here, wondering what the hell I'm going to do to get this article going. I've got a Tuesday deadline, 5 articles lined up, all with national magazines, and I'm fiddling with things on my desk instead of writing the words and collecting the cash. Hey, I like that line. Okay, I'm freewriting, so let's see what I can say about the bloody subject. First, I guess the problem right now is that I have two parts of me, doing battle over what I should write. One is telling me that what I've just written two words ago is trash, and that I should stop, carefully consider it, and then maybe ic write it, or maybe even that I'm an incompetent writer, and that I should give it up if this is the best that I can do with it. Jesus, but I'm not going to stop now, no matter what, because that is exactly what that first character, the editor, wants me to do. To be sure, I need that editor, when the time is right, but for the first draft, I'm doing just fine by letting the writer take control, and telling the editor to take a hike. He's there, now, telling me to stop, reminding me of the ache in my fingers, telling me that my shoulders are sore from all this typing, and just how long can I keep on typing anyway, hunh? It is especially tempting at the end of sentences to stop, since that is a natural resting place. But do I give in? Not till I've got this section written, typos, aching shoulders and everything. Once I've got this section written, then I can stop, sip at my nice, herb tea, and let the editor carefully consider the stuff I've put down, and let that little dicken refine it. Except,

I've got a great idea: one that will drive that little guy absolutely bonkers: I'm not going to let that editor refine this, I'll include it in the article as a sample of freewriting, and let the readers see what goes on in a typical freewriting session. And that, I think, is where I'm going to stop, because now I have something on the page, and a good hook for this section of the article, and maybe for the article as a whole. There, you little rascal!

I stay pretty much on topic in this particular passage. It doesn't always work out this well. Sometimes it comes down to either straying off topic or writing nothing at all. In that situation, the writer goes for whatever keeps him writing, even something like:

"Goo-goo, ga-ga, I feel like a baby, just making stupid sounds to keep from stopping, but whatever I need to do to keep on going, I will. Now, what was my topic again? Oh yeah—the Mexican pickle industry as a major force in world agriculture."

In focused freewriting, nonsense is a placeholder, something to keep you writing until you can regain your focus.

Why is it so important to continue writing, no matter what you actually put down on paper? As mentioned in the passage, there really are two aspects to the writing self: the creator and the editor. As one of my writing professors once said, the creator puts the *clay* on the table, that basic stuff that can then be shaped by the editor. But until the clay *is* on the table, the editor is a hindrance, trying to get you to stop before you've even started.

The editor is a perfectionist and will not accept anything that is less than perfect. The creator, however, needs the freedom to put down *everything*, including the non-perfect and maybe even the downright lousy. *Then*, and *only* then is the editor needed and welcome.

Freewriting works by keeping the editor distracted by the sheer *volume* and *speed* of writing. Your particular "editor" may be strong enough to distract you from writing anything worthwhile, so that initially you write paragraph after paragraph of nonsense or banality. Keep going. I was stuck, recently, on an article for *Harper's* magazine. I ended up freewriting for half an hour. The result was the best article I have ever done for one of the most prestigious magazines in the world. Now if only my editor hadn't quit the magazine, that article might have been published!

You'll notice too, that the freewriting passage above gave me more than writing material. It gave me a *slant*, that of incorporating an actual pre-writing sample into the body of the article.

Freewriting can give you more than just a jump-start. Sometimes, it can give you an entire first draft. A few weeks ago, I was assigned to do a story on an airport. I went to the airport and took copious notes on everything I could find, poking about in dusty corners and describing in detail the various girly calendars and posters on the walls. I filled seemingly countless pages in my notebook.

When I got home, I was about to review my notes, when, on impulse, I decided to do a focused freewriting, just to warm up. Instead of *warming* up, I *finished* up, writing the entire article in one half-hour freewriting session. I never did use those notes, except to confirm a statistic or quote. *That* article *was* published and was well received, as was the check the magazine sent me. Not bad for half an hour of "nonsense writing."

What if you don't have even a *topic* in mind? Then comes penstorming.

PREWRITING TECHNIQUE #2: PENSTORMING

I first came across penstorming during a financial workshop I attended many years ago. The workshop leader had us take pen in hand and begin writing. There were no rules or instructions, other than we were not to stop, even for a moment, until she told us to. In essence, then, it was freewriting without even the restriction of remaining focused on a particular topic. At the end of fifteen minutes, there wasn't a person in that room who wasn't astounded at the revelations and perceptions staring up at them from the page.

Penstorming might seem too chaotic to produce anything worthwhile to a writer. In fact, however, the complete freedom which penstorming allows is what makes it such a valuable technique, especially for writers looking for topics on which to write.

In freewriting, the restriction of staying on topic helps the writer to produce something specific to the article he is writing, but restricts him from discovering *new* topics. Penstorming allows the writer to roam about at will, from the sublime to the ridiculous, from topic to topic.

Freewriting and penstorming work on the principle that we *always* have something worthwhile to say. Sometimes, however, a part of our conscious mind called the *Critical Censor* prevents worthwhile ideas from emerging from the subconscious.

Penstorming keeps the Critical Censor so busy with the physical writing process itself that those valuable ideas just slip right onto the page. Before you know it, there it is, staring up at you from the previously barren page: the synopsis of *Everything You Wanted To Know About Saudi Arabia But Were Afraid of Having To Become a Muslim To Find Out.*

A word of warning: Penstorming (and sometimes focused freewriting) can release many things from our subconscious, things which we are not always anxious to recall or discover. If it is any consolation, these sometimes horrible little bits often form the basis of truly powerful writing. While writing the piece for *Harper's*, I used focused freewriting and found myself dredging up extraordinarily painful memories, memories which I had not attended to in twenty years or more. Instead of suppressing the horror, I allowed myself to feel it in full, then incorporated it into the article. The result was several moving passages which raised the article to a new level and which later became part of an award-winning screenplay.

PREWRITING TECHNIQUE #3: STYLE COPYING

If you're looking for a warm-up rather than a jump-start, style copying can serve quite well. Style copying entails copying passages, verbatim, from the work of accomplished writers. The point isn't to commit plagiarism, but rather to get a feel for writing excellence.

Professional athletes have long known that emulation is the surest method of achieving excellence. Tennis players watch training films, practice the perfect swing ad nauseam, and sit with eyes closed, visualizing that winning forehand smash.

Self-improvement experts espouse the benefits of surrounding yourself with the things you want: Test-drive that Mercedes, try on that beautiful coat, read those magazines on wealth and success, and before long they will be yours.

So it is with style copying: Emulate perfection often enough, and soon you are experiencing that perfection in your own writing. Kind of like the old cliché, "Fake it 'til you make it." You may not be aware of an improvement in your writing, but when you get to that tricky point-of-view problem, you might breeze right through it, adapting a technique you encountered during style copying.

PREWRITING TECHNIQUE #4: WHO'S ON FIRST?

Journalists swear by "the five Ws and the H": Who, When, What, Where, Why, and How.

This technique ensures that all aspects of a news story are covered, from what happened to who was involved. The real news is that this technique is invaluable in *any* kind of writing, from novels to non-fiction and even poetry. After all, writing (any type of writing) is meant to convey information.

Using "the five Ws and the H" ensures that a story contains all the information the reader needs. Even if readers do not *consciously* identify each of the elements involved in a story, there will be a feeling of dissatisfaction if they don't find out *who* was caught flashing *which* member of the royal family, *why* character X is in Morocco trying to find character Y, or *what* the focus of your poem really is.

The "five Ws and the H" can also be used as a pre-writing technique. If you have a topic in mind, you can use this technique to focus and develop that topic. Once you know *who* the article, story, or poem is about, and *what, how, when, where,* and *why* an incident occurred, you have a solid frame on which to hang your story.

If you have yet to select a topic, you can plug random elements into each of the questions until you come up with the right idea. This, of course, is an elaboration of the old "What if?" technique.

Thus, you can use this technique both before and after writing your first draft: before, to come up with the idea or framework; after, to ensure that you have the proper information and focus.

APPENDIX B: ADaPTiNG NoVeLS TO THE SCREEN

I'm primarily a screenwriter these days. But I began as a novelist, and in the course of my screenwriting career, I have adapted two of my own novels, as well as another author's bestselling novel, for a prominent production company. All three projects died in Development Hell, but I learned a few things along the way that may be useful if you are asked to adapt a novel for the big (or small) screen.

The way you adapt a particular novel depends on whether you're adapting your own work or someone else's novel. If you're adapting someone else's work, some choices may be decided for you ahead of time by the person paying you, or by the novelist.

For example, you may feel that one character is the natural hero, while the novelist or producer may see a different character as the hero. You may even feel that one of the novel's storylines is the "real" story that needs to be told, but your employer and/or the novelist is convinced that the main storyline is the storyline you're not even interested in.

There is no "rule" about this. If you have enough influence, you may be able to change your employer's mind. Otherwise, they're paying the piper so you'll have to play their tune or they'll find some other piper to pay—and to order around.

A novel is much larger than a script and often contains more than one hero or opponent and multiple storylines in many locations, even multiple time periods. It's necessary to choose from among these various elements.

Another possible difficulty is the use of prose as the major element in a novel; the medium becomes the message. A beautifully written novel about nothing can still be a commercially viable book simply because of the beauty of the language itself. You can have a stream of consciousness novel that involves nothing but interior monologues, philosophy, psychology, symbolism, internal angst, regret — none of which will show well on screen.

NOTE: The beauty of the prose alone can sell a book, but not a movie.

A great example is *Brokeback Mountain*. When I read the script, my first reaction was that it was pretty good (not brilliant, not great, but pretty good). Then I saw the film and I was surprised at how weak it was. I had to re-read the script to realize that a lot of the power of the writing was in the narration, not in dialogue or action. Narration doesn't make it onto the screen unless you have a voice-over, which is difficult to pull off. In addition, the directing was weak, again surprising because of Ang Lee's reputation and past successes.

In the script, the narrative included descriptions of what the characters were really like. It emphasized facial expressions and subtle reactions. In effect, it took the place of dialogue. (The film has very little dialogue for a feature film.) One of the authors, the legendary Larry McMurtry (*Terms of Endearment, Lonesome Dove, Hud*, and *The Last Picture Show* among others) admitted it was a film about people (cowboys) who don't talk much. (Now there's a great clue as to the viability of a story: no dialogue!) They don't emote much. They don't communicate much. So McMurtry and his partner Diana Ossana made up for it with narrative.

Now that might work well in silent films or for mime. But in a modern-day feature film? Well … maybe not.

Yes, the film was nominated for an Oscar, the most prestigious award a film can win. Yes, the screenwriters won for Best Screenplay. However, the film did very poorly at the box office and the Oscar nod was based as much on the film's controversial, politically correct theme of homosexual love as it was on quality. I seriously doubt that this film, with a man and woman as the leads, would even have gotten made, much less been nominated. The film wasn't about people; it was about an issue.

The point is that you need to give your audience something to see and something to listen to. Like I mentioned earlier in the book, if there was a woman who was sitting on a rock, contemplating her life, it may be an intensely moving internal scene— but that doesn't make it a dynamic film. For a novel to translate to the big screen, it has to be full of action.

My favorite examples of the introspective kind of writing that usually does not make it to the big screen are the novels by Thomas Wolfe, *Look Homeward, Angel*, and *You Can't Go Home Again*. The power of these brilliant books rests in the brilliance of the narrative because, believe me, nothing happens. Again, you can get away with that in a novel, but not in a screenplay—unless, apparently, you're Larry McMurtry and at least two of your characters are gay.

Stephen King's novels are more suited to the screen than are Wolfe's, Pynchon's, or even Nobel Prize winners Steinbeck's or Faulkner's. That's because King's works are visual, have a strong central storyline, and are wrapped around one clearly delineated protagonist and usually one clearly delineated antagonist.

NOTE: Complex novels, or novels that depend on the power of the author's prose, rarely make it to the screen. And if they do, they tend not to do well.

Think of how many comic books are made into movies compared to how many Pulitzer prize-winning novels are adapted for the screen, and you'll get the idea.

The potboiler gothic romance novel *Gone With the Wind* and the Harry Potter children's books are immeasurably more successful than the powerful but dark and sophisticated writings of the great Russian novelists. What would you rather get royalties from: Chekhov's *The Cherry Orchard* or Stan Lee's *Spiderman* movies?

So, first determine if your novel is suited to adaptation. If it's a 300,000-word, prose-heavy novel with multiple storylines and a cast of thousands, it might not be viable for adaptation.

Here's a test: Can you create a logline for your novel?

If you can't write a logline for the novel you want to adapt, you may be having trouble identifying the main elements—maybe there are too many of them—or too few of them (some elements missing).

Begin your logline by identifying the novel's main elements. It may entail creating "amalgam characters" and "amalgam storylines"—in other words, combining various redundant story elements.

If your novel has several protagonists, you may also have several life-changing events, several opponents, several allies, etc. You must choose which of those events drives the story that you want to tell. That's an important point—you are in some ways telling a story that's different from the one told in the novel. Or, at the very least, you are telling only one of several stories told in the novel.

NOTE: You may end up with a very different story. Don't be afraid of this possibility. However, make those changes only in order to convey the story on the big screen as effectively as possible.

The bottom line is that you need to do whatever is necessary to make the novelist's story work on screen. This depends, again, on how much latitude the novelist and/or producer has given you.

Good luck and remember: If it's a choice between Spidey and Agamemnon, go with the webhead.

The previous article originally appeared in *Scriptmag*.
